Editor
Lorin Klistoff, M.A.

Managing Editor
Karen J. Goldfluss, M.S. Ed.

Cover Artist
Brenda DiAntonis

Art Coordinator
Renée Christine Yates

Art Production Manager
Kevin Barnes

Imaging
James Edward Grace
Ricardo Martinez

Publisher
Mary D. Smith, M.S. Ed.

DAILY WARM-UPS
Reading
GRADE 2

- Over 150 nonfiction and fiction pass...
- Follow-up questions for each pass... target essential comprehension sk...
- Ideal for test preparation!

Author

Shelle Russell

Teacher Created Resources, Inc.
6421 Industry Way
Westminster, CA 92683
www.teachercreated.com

ISBN: 978-1-4206-3488-4

©2006 Teacher Created Resources, Inc.
Reprinted, 2011
Made in U.S.A.

Table of Contents

The Giraffe—Cats—Squid—Puffins—Saola—Mole Rat—Tiger—Lions—Red
Squirrel—Night Animals—Chipmunk—Sharks—Hermit Crab—Tongues—
Groundhogs—Seahorses—Ostrich—Hummingbirds

George Washington—Betsy Ross—Thomas Jefferson—Dolley Madison—
Albert Einstein—George W. Bush—Michelle Kwan—Tiger Woods—
Condoleeza Rice—Walt Disney—Denzel Washington—Sandra Bullock—
Bruce Willis—Laura Bush—Babe Ruth—Hank Aaron—Christopher
Columbus—Harriet Tubman

Airplane—Cell Phones—Coke—The Iron—The Popsicle—Light Bulbs—
Kool-Aid—Marshmallows—Microwave Oven—Q-tips—Sewing Machine—
Umbrellas—Wipers—Band-Aids—Basketball—The Telephone—Braille—
Diapers

Mammals—Birds—Fish—Reptiles—Amphibians—Insects—Seeds—
Habitats—Seasons—Earth's Resources

Winter Olympics—iPod—Hurricane Katrina—Tsunami—Tour de France—
September 11th—John Paul II Dies—Ben—Air Force One—Lion King
Tryouts—Five Mummies—Working in the Mines—Moms and Dads Want
Kids To Eat Veggies—Space Shuttle Comes Home

Table of Contents

Introduction

The goal of this book is to help children improve their skills in both reading and comprehension on a daily basis. The more experience a child has with reading, the stronger his or her reading and problem-solving skills will become. *Daily Warm Ups: Reading (Grade 2)* is composed of short passages which provide both factual and fictional material. Questions which follow are based on Bloom's Taxonomy, higher-level thinking skills, and national standards which are required for grade two learners. Using this book in your daily routine will boost children's reading and comprehension scores significantly.

Nonfiction and Fiction

Daily Warm Ups: Reading is divided into two sections: fiction (narrative) and nonfiction (expository). Each of the two sections is divided into five categories. The nonfiction section includes the following: animals, biographies, American history, science, and current events. The fiction section includes the following: fairy tales and folklore, historical fiction, contemporary fiction, mystery/adventure/suspense, and fantasy.

Because understanding both types of literature is extremely important to our student's success, exposure to both fiction and nonfiction reading is essential. Questions which follow the passages are strategically written to address concepts and strategies which are required nationwide.

Comprehension Questions

Comprehension is the most important goal of any reading assignment. Students who comprehend what they read perform better in class, score higher on tests, and perform tasks in life more confidently. Questions that follow the reading passages are written to encourage students to recognize structure of the text, visualize, summarize, learn new vocabulary, and implement strategies for breaking words into parts for better comprehension. Reading skills used in *Daily Warm-Ups: Reading* can also be found in scope and sequence charts across the nation. Different types of questions are written to help students become more confident in the following:

• Comparing/contrasting	• Understanding vocabulary
• Recognizing facts/opinions	• Recalling details
• Synonyms/antonyms	• Identify types of sentences
• Author purpose	• Making simple inferences/predictions
• Multi-meaning words	• Homophones/long and short vowels
• Recognizing main idea	• Blends/ compound words
• Word structure (prefix/suffix)	• Describing character traits

Introduction

Readability

Each of the reading passages in *Daily Warm-Ups: Reading (Grade 2)* varies in difficulty to meet the various reading levels of your students. The passages have been categorized as follows: below grade level, at grade level, and above grade level. (See Leveling Chart on page 175.)

Record Keeping

Use the tracking sheet on page 6 to record which warm-up exercises you have given to your students. Or, distribute copies of the sheet for students to keep their own records. Use the certificate on page 176 as you see fit. You can use the certificate as a reward for students completing a certain number of warm-up exercises. Or, you may choose to distribute the certificates to students who complete the warm-up exercises with 100% accuracy.

How to Make the Most of This Book

Here are some simple tips, which you may have already thought of, already implemented, or may be new to you. They are only suggestions to help you make your students as successful in reading as possible.

- Read through the book ahead of time so you are familiar with each portion. The better you understand how the book works, the easier it will be to answer students' questions.

- Set aside a regular time each day to incorporate Daily Warm-Ups into your routine. Once the routine is established, students will look forward to and expect to work on reading strategies at that particular time.

- Make sure that any amount of time spent on Daily Warm-Ups is positive and constructive. This should be a time of practicing for success and recognizing it as it is achieved.

- Allot only about five minutes to Daily Warm-Ups. Too much time will not be useful, too little time will create additional stress.

- Be sure to model the reading and question answering process at the beginning of the year before students attempt to do the passages on their own. Modeling for about five days in a row seems to be a good start. Model pre-reading questions, reading the passage, highlighting information which refers to the questions, and eliminating answers which are obviously wrong. Finally, refer back to the text once again, to make sure the answers chosen are the best ones.

- Create and store overheads of each lesson so that you can review student work, concepts, and strategies as quickly as possible.

- Utilize peer tutors which have strong skills for peer interaction to assist with struggling students.

- Offer small group time to students which need extra enrichment or opportunities for questions regarding the text. Small groups will allow many of these students, once they are comfortable with the format, to achieve success independently.

- Adjust the procedures, as you see fit, to meet the needs of all your students.

Tracking Sheet

NONFICTION

Animals		Biography		American History		Science		Current Events	
Page 9		Page 27		Page 45		Page 63		Page 73	
Page 10		Page 28		Page 46		Page 64		Page 74	
Page 11		Page 29		Page 47		Page 65		Page 75	
Page 12		Page 30		Page 48		Page 66		Page 76	
Page 13		Page 31		Page 49		Page 67		Page 77	
Page 14		Page 32		Page 50		Page 68		Page 78	
Page 15		Page 33		Page 51		Page 69		Page 79	
Page 16		Page 34		Page 52		Page 70		Page 80	
Page 17		Page 35		Page 53		Page 71		Page 81	
Page 18		Page 36		Page 54		Page 72		Page 82	
Page 19		Page 37		Page 55				Page 83	
Page 20		Page 38		Page 56				Page 84	
Page 21		Page 39		Page 57				Page 85	
Page 22		Page 40		Page 58				Page 86	
Page 23		Page 41		Page 59					
Page 24		Page 42		Page 60					
Page 25		Page 43		Page 61					
Page 26		Page 44		Page 62					

FICTION

Fairy Tales and Folklore		Historical Fiction		Contemporary Realistic Fiction		Mystery/Suspense/ Adventure		Fantasy	
Page 89		Page 105		Page 121		Page 137		Page 151	
Page 90		Page 106		Page 122		Page 138		Page 152	
Page 91		Page 107		Page 123		Page 139		Page 153	
Page 92		Page 108		Page 124		Page 140		Page 154	
Page 93		Page 109		Page 125		Page 141		Page 155	
Page 94		Page 110		Page 126		Page 142		Page 156	
Page 95		Page 111		Page 127		Page 143		Page 157	
Page 96		Page 112		Page 128		Page 144		Page 158	
Page 97		Page 113		Page 129		Page 145		Page 159	
Page 98		Page 114		Page 130		Page 146		Page 160	
Page 99		Page 115		Page 131		Page 147		Page 161	
Page 100		Page 116		Page 132		Page 148		Page 162	
Page 101		Page 117		Page 133		Page 149		Page 163	
Page 102		Page 118		Page 134		Page 150		Page 164	
Page 103		Page 119		Page 135				Page 165	
Page 104		Page 120		Page 136				Page 166	

NONFICTION

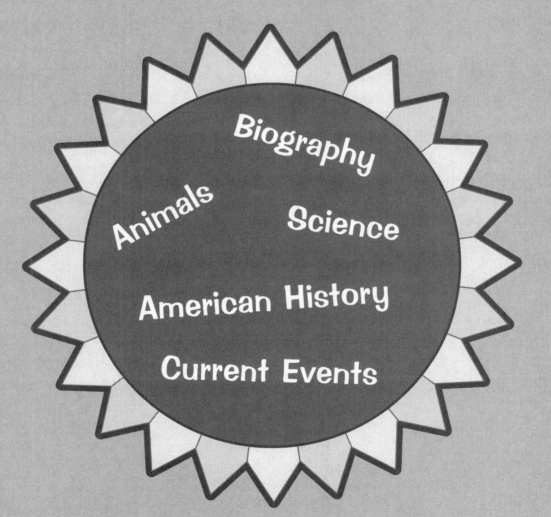

Biography

Animals

Science

American History

Current Events

Name _____ **Date** _____

THE GIRAFFE

The giraffe has a tall, long neck that helps the giraffe get food from high places. The giraffe can bite leaves off of the top of a tree, and it can <u>munch</u> flowers on a roof.

A male will fight with his neck. This is called neck fighting. Two males hit each other with their heads, and they fight until they get tired. The giraffe that stops the fight wins.

A giraffe also uses his neck to keep safe. His long neck helps him to see danger when it is out in the grass. The giraffe watches for lions and other dangerous animals. The mother giraffe can be eating far away and can still keep an eye on her babies. She holds her head high and keeps looking around.

To stay alive, giraffes have to stand tall!

STORY QUESTIONS

1. What body part helps the giraffe eat leaves on the tops of trees?
   a. head   c. feet
   b. neck   d. ears

2. This story is mostly about . . .
   a. a lion.
   b. a mother.
   c. the giraffe.
   d. a baby.

3. A **synonym** is a word that means the same thing. *Munch* means . . .
   a. watch
   b. eat
   c. look
   d. stand

Name _____ **Date** _____

CATS

Cats have things that help them catch mice. These things also help cats get away.

Cats use these to feel their way in the dark, and they use them to find out how large a hole is. They also use these when the air moves. These things help tell the cat if there is a wall, a bed, or an object from the air that hits them. The cat uses these to feel its food on the ground. They tell the cat if a mouse is about to get away. If a twig hits it, the cat will blink to protect its eyes because these things let it know quickly that something is coming toward it.

Do you know what part of a cat this is? It is the whiskers! They give the cat feeling. They guide and save the cat from getting hurt. They help your cat go through its <u>day</u> and night happy.

STORY QUESTIONS

1. What is this story mostly about?
   a. keeping your cat safe
   b. the life of a cat
   c. a cat's whiskers
   d. helping your cat eat the right food

2. An **antonym** means the opposite. *Day* is an antonym for . . .
   a. light.   c. big.
   b. wall.   d. night.

3. Which one is **NOT TRUE** about the cat's whiskers?
   a. They help it to cook rice.
   b. They save the cat from getting hurt.
   c. They help it find their way in the dark.
   d. They help it catch mice.

Name _____ **Date** _____

SQUID

Do you know which is one of the biggest animals in the ocean?

It is the squid. A squid had eight arms. It has two longer arms called tentacles. Its arms are as long <u>as a school bus</u>. The squid also has eyes that are as big as a basketball.

Squid like to eat small fish and small squid. They use their long arms to grab the fish. The eight arms help to keep the fish from getting away. Last, they put the fish or small squid in their mouths. Their beaks are sharp, and they cut the fish to pieces.

There are still many things to learn about the squid. They live so far down in the ocean that it makes it hard to learn about them.

STORY QUESTIONS

1. What is the name for the arms of the squid?
   a. eight
   b. mouth
   c. tentacles
   d. beak

2. In the text, "as long as a school bus" means . . .
   a. the arms move in the water like a bus.
   b. the arms have doors like a bus.
   c. the arms look like a school bus.
   d. the arms are very long like a school bus.

3. Why is it hard to learn much about the squid?
   a. It lives so far down under the water.
   b. It moves too fast.
   c. It is hard to catch with all those arms.
   d. Its beak is too sharp.

PUFFINS

Puffins are little birds that look a lot like penguins. They have black feathers and a black head. Their tummies are made up of white feathers. They have white faces and yellow, orange, and black beaks. Puffins are like <u>tiny fluffy balls</u> when they first hatch.

They like to live in groups. Puffins never live alone. They love to be with other puffins. They live in places that have rocks by the water. They build nests in the rocks with small pieces of feathers and twigs. When they are not in their nests, they are swimming in the ocean.

Momma puffins catch small fish to feed the babies. They go out and catch the fish and bring it back to the nest to feed. They do not have baby puffins until they are five years old.

Puffins are pretty birds. They have to live in groups to be happy.

STORY QUESTIONS

1. What is the meaning of "tiny fluffy balls" from the text?
   a. They look like big clouds.
   b. Their bodies are small and soft like cotton balls.
   c. They are huge and can not move.
   d. They look like fat balls of snow.

2. This story tells you . . .
   a. how a puffin lives.
   b. things a puffin eats.
   c. many facts about puffins.
   d. what puffins like to do on a rainy day.

3. A new title for this might be . . .
   a. "Puffin Facts."   c. "My Pet Puffin."
   b. "A Day with a Fat Puffin."   d. "Puffins by the Rocks."

SAOLA

Scientists <u>found</u> a new animal in 1992 in Vietnam. They did not know about the Saola before. Saola (sah-oh-la) means long wooden sticks.

A Saola looks like a deer and loves to hide in the forest. It has long, straight horns. These horns look like giant toothpicks. They are from 12 to 20 inches long.

The Saola is short. It weighs about 220 pounds. The Saola has white lines on its face. Its hair is short and brown. The Saola's eyes are very big. It has a dark black strip down under its fluffy tail.

People do not know very much about the Saola. The people who hunt them make traps or send dogs to catch them.

Saola is a new animal that has been found in the world. Will there be more?

STORY QUESTIONS

1. When the author added an "s" to *horn* (*horns*), what did it mean?
   a. The Saola has more than one horn.
   b. The Saola has no horns.
   c. The Saola has only one horn.

2. A **synonym** is a word that means the same thing. *Found* means . . .
   a. put in a new place.
   b. did not have.
   c. lost.
   d. discovered.

3. What do the horns of the Saola look like?
   a. small candy bars
   b. long wooden sticks
   c. giant toothpicks
   d. long pens or pencils

DAILY
Warm-Up 6

Name _____   Date _____

MOLE RAT

Mole rats are strange. They have no fur, but live in the ground. Mole rats look like rats, and they live like bees or ants. They have very sharp teeth. The teeth are located in the front of their mouths. Two teeth are on top, and two teeth are on the bottom.

They live with many other mole rats. One mole rat has babies, and she is the <u>queen</u>. She can have up to one hundred babies a year. The other mole rats bring her food. They make sure she is safe, and they care for her babies.

All of the mole rats have jobs. Small mole rats find food and keep the tunnel clean. The big mole rats dig. The biggest mole rats make sure the mole rats are safe.

Mole rats dig and dig. Scientists think they dig to look for roots to eat. Some mole rats can now be seen in zoos.

STORY QUESTIONS

1. According to the text, what is a mole rat?
   a. an animal that looks like a rat, but lives like a bee or an ant
   b. an animal that looks like a bird, but acts like a dog
   c. an animal that looks like a cat, but acts like a bird

2. Using the words around it, other words for *queen* would be . . .
   a. the mole rat that takes care of the babies.
   b. the mole rat that cleans out the nest.
   c. the mole rat that finds food.
   d. the mole rat that is the boss.

3. Homophones are words that sound alike, but mean different things. Which one is used correctly?
   a. <u>Sum</u> of the holes are small.
   b. <u>Some</u> of the mole rats dig for roots.
   c. <u>Sum</u> mole rats can be seen in the zoo.

DAILY Warm-Up 7   Name _____   Date _____

TIGER

Did you know that <u>tigers</u> look like big cats? Most of them live in the wild; however, some people buy them for pets. Other people look at them in the zoo.

If tigers become pets, the people who own them are still not always safe. Tigers will purr like a cat, and they will lick your arm. Sometimes they will go where you go. They love to play, but they are still wild animals. People who have tigers for pets need to remember that tigers can still get mad and cannot be trusted. Tigers can <u>bite</u>. If they put their ears flat, do not go near them. If they curl their lips, it is not safe to be near them.

At the zoo, the tigers live in a cage. People can walk by and look at them. The people who look at them cannot pet them or feed them. The tigers can walk in their cage, and they can lie in the sun. People can see the orange and black on their coats, and they can hear them growl. As long as the people stay outside of the cage, they are safe.

Just remember that whether you see a tiger in the wild, as a pet, or in the zoo, the tiger may look pretty, but it is not safe.

STORY QUESTIONS

1. Where do most tigers live?
   - a. in the zoo
   - b. with people as pets
   - c. in the wild
   - d. at the park

2. The word *bite* could be changed to . . .
   - a. "make a loud noise."
   - b. "walk in their cage."
   - c. "put their teeth into."
   - d. "swim in the water."

3. The word *tigers* means . . .
   - a. more than one tiger.
   - b. one tiger.
   - c. no tiger.

Name _____ Date _____

LIONS

Baby lions take a long time to grow up. Baby lions cannot hunt for themselves. For the first two years of their life, the mother lion finds food for them. They eat food that other animals have killed. They even steal food. The mother lion also teaches them how to stay safe.

When they are two years old, they go away from home. It is now time to find homes of their own. They know how to hunt, and they know how to find a place to live. It is time to make their new homes.

The lions will stay in this place, and they will have babies of their own. The mother lion will teach her new babies to hunt and find food. She will also teach them to stay safe. Her babies will turn two years old, and then they will leave to have families of their own.

STORY QUESTIONS

1. How long do the lions stay with their mother?
   a. 10 years
   b. 3 years
   c. 2 years
   d. 5 years

2. Before they are two years old, how do the babies get food?
   a. The mother lion finds food for them.
   b. They kill it.
   c. The man in the zoo gives it to them.
   d. The man with the yellow hat brings it to them.

3. Why do the babies stay with their mother for so long?
   a. so they can play and roll in the grass
   b. so they can learn to hunt and take care of themselves
   c. so they can talk to her

RED SQUIRREL

Have you ever seen a red squirrel? It is furry. Its hair is brown, gray, and white. It is short, and it has very sharp claws. It has teeth in the front of its mouth. The teeth are long and sharp. Its eyes are as black as coal. The ears are very little and sit on the back of the head.

When the baby is born, it <u>has no hair and is blind</u>. The mother has a nest in a tree or somewhere that is safe. The mother feeds the baby milk. She stays with it unless she is looking for food.

By the summer, the babies can see well. They have fur and are bigger. The babies can play out of the nest. They learn to find seeds, insects, and mushrooms.

When winter comes to the woods, babies can live alone. They have thick coats that are warm. They now know how to look for food and can build nests of their own.

STORY QUESTIONS

1. When we read this story, we can guess that the red squirrel is . . .
   a. a busy animal.
   b. a lazy animal.
   c. an angry animal.
   d. an animal that likes to play games.

2. In the last paragraph, the author is telling you about . . .
   a. the squirrel's eyes.
   b. how the squirrel drinks the mother's milk.
   c. how the squirrel finds seeds and plants.
   d. how the squirrel is ready to live all alone.

3. The words "has no hair and is blind" mean . . .
   a. the baby has no coat to stay warm.
   b. the baby does not have any hair and it cannot see.
   c. the baby does not have sun glasses.

Name _____   Date _____

NIGHT ANIMALS

Some animals hunt and look for mates at night while other animals sleep. To hunt at night, they have to hear very well. They have to see and smell well, too. They have to be able to touch well.

Owls have eyes that help them see in the dark. Foxes have large ears to help grab sounds. Their ears move to find out where the sounds come from. Cats use their whiskers to help them feel their way in the dark. Raccoons use their front paws to catch fish and frogs. They put their hands in the water and feel for the fish. Bats make high sounds. The sounds then bounce back to their ears. The sound is called an echo. It helps them tell where objects are.

Night animals have to use their senses to find food and mates.

STORY QUESTIONS

1. Which one is **NOT** a fact about night animals?
   a. All night animals sleep in the night.
   b. Some night animals can see in the dark.
   c. Some night animals hunt in the night.
   d. Night animals use their senses to help them find food.

2. What does a fox use to hear sounds?
   a. his long tail
   b. his large ears
   c. his long nose
   d. his big eyes

3. **Homophones** are words that sound alike but have different meanings. Which one is used correctly?
   a. Can you tell me <u>wear</u> to look for the bat?
   b. <u>Wear</u> are the animals?
   c. I would like to <u>where</u> my shoes.
   d. The echo tells the bat <u>where</u> to go.

CHIPMUNK

Have you ever seen a chipmunk with extremely fat cheeks? The fat cheeks have pouches in them. They are like pockets to place food in. The fat cheeks make it easy to carry food back to its home. When their cheeks get filled, they start to puff outwards.

All day the chipmunks run around and look for food in the woods. They look for items such as acorns and other nuts. Seeds and berries are also things they like to eat. They nibble and munch all day long.

Chipmunks have very long toes with sharp nails. Their tails are long, black, and furry. Their ears are small, and they have black stripes running down their backs. Their fur is tan and their belly is white.

Chipmunks are a lot of fun to watch when they play. If they are stuffing their cheeks, it is the most fun of all.

STORY QUESTIONS

1. An **opinion** is something that you think. Which one is an opinion about a chipmunk?

　a. They stuff food in their cheeks.　　c. They have long, furry tails.

　b. They eat seeds and berries.　　d. They are cute.

2. What **compound word** could be added to the text above?

　a. overcoat

　b. paperclip

　c. toenail

　d. baseball

3. If you wanted to make a new title, it might be . . .

　a. "The Busy Life of a Chipmunk."

　b. "My Friend Chippy."

　c. "How Chipmunks Eat Seeds."

DAILY
Warm-Up 12

Name _____ Date _____

SHARKS

Sharks are one kind of fish. They live deep in the ocean where it is very cold. Sharks can be very large.

They do not have bones. They have cartilage. It is the same thing you have in your nose and ears. They have tiny slits in the side of their heads. These slits help them to breathe air. Their teeth are very sharp. Extra teeth are hidden inside. Sometimes they lose one tooth, and a new one will grow right back in. Some huge sharks can grow teeth that are as big as a hand.

Sharks like to eat meat, fish, and plants. Some sharks swim with their mouths open to catch plants. The plants stick to the sides of their mouths. Others eat seals or small animals in the ocean.

If you want to see a shark, the best and safest place is at the aquarium!

STORY QUESTIONS

1. If sharks do not have bones, what keeps them together?
   a. cartilage
   b. teeth
   c. bones
   d. hands

2. This passage is written in . . .
   a. no person at all
   b. first person
   c. second person
   d. third person

3. Where is the safest place to see a shark?
   a. park
   b. circus
   c. aquarium

20

Name _____ Date _____

HERMIT CRAB

Have you ever gone to the beach? Have you seen a hermit crab? You might not know what they look like. You might not know where they live.

Hermit crabs are strange-looking animals. They have a round head that is soft. Hermit crabs have long legs that help them to move very fast. The legs have a lot of parts. Some hermit crabs are red while others can be brown or orange. Some hermit crabs are more than one color. Most of the time there are little hairs that stick out of their shells.

The hermit crabs do not have hard shells like other crabs. They have to find empty shells in the ocean to live in. When they grow, they find a new shell that is larger. These shells help to keep them safe. The hermit crab uses his claws to act like a door when it is inside a shell. It also uses its claw to grab food when it is hungry.

Hermit crabs are not like other crabs. They live in others' shells. This makes them special.

STORY QUESTIONS

1. Which compound word above means "to be in something"?
   a. outside
   b. hermit
   c. inside
   d. empty

2. In the passage, the word *grab* can be changed to . . .
   a. "take a hold of."
   b. "throw."
   c. "toss."
   d. "play ball."

3. What do hermit crabs do that other crabs do not do?
   a. live far out in the ocean
   b. live inside any shell they can find
   c. swim faster than the other crabs
   d. walk slower than any other crab

DAILY Warm-Up 14   **Name** _____   **Date** _____

TONGUES

Animals' tongues are used for many things. A fox does not sweat when it is hot. It puts its tongue out of its mouth and pants. When he pants, it means he breathes in and out very fast. This is the way the fox keeps cool.

Lions use their tongues to keep their fur clean. Their tongues are rough. It works like a brush on their fur.

Geckos use their tongues to lick their eyes. They do not have eyelids, so the tongue helps them to keep their eyes clean.

Chameleons use their tongue to catch insects. Their tongues are long and sticky. It makes hunting easy.

If a goose does not want someone around, it sticks out its tongue and makes a hissing noise.

Snakes have long, thin tongues. They are <u>split</u> in the middle. They use their tongues to smell for mice and other small prey.

Did you know animals used their tongues in so many ways?

STORY QUESTIONS

1. Synonyms are words that mean the same thing. <u>Split</u> is a synonym for . . .
   a. sew.   c. clean.
   b. cut.   d. make.

2. What can chameleons do with their tongues?
   a. play a game
   b. eat large animals
   c. catch bugs
   d. lick their eyes

3. Which word from the text can used in more than one way?
   a. tongue   c. pants
   b. did   d. smell

DAILY Warm-Up 15 Name _____ Date _____

GROUNDHOGS

Groundhogs are exciting animals. They are rodents like rats and mice, and they love to do many things.

First, they love to eat and eat. All day long they love to eat. Groundhogs eat plants and flowers. They eat fruits and veggies.

A groundhog will have dirt on his nose a lot. Why? The dirt is from digging under the ground. They dig holes all over underground. These holes are called tunnels. Groundhogs live in the holes. They pile up food in the holes. In the winter, they sleep inside, and the tunnels keep them safe and warm.

When it is spring, they have babies. The babies are called pups. The pups play games, and the mother watches them. She makes a loud noise if the pups are in danger. The pups run back to the burrow so they will be safe.

They are fun to watch when they play and when they dig. Groundhogs are always busy digging or playing!

STORY QUESTIONS

1. Which compound word is **NOT** used in this passage?
   a. groundhogs
   b. inside
   c. outside
   d. underground

2. What is the name for something that groundhogs dig?
   a. tunnel
   b. danger
   c. pups
   d. food

3. Which one of the sentences is a fact?
   a. Groundhogs are as big as a cat.
   b. Groundhogs love to dig in the dirt.
   c. Groundhogs are orange and black.

DAILY Name _____ Date _____
Warm-Up 16

SEAHORSES

Did you know that a seahorse is a special kind of fish? Did you know it lives in the ocean?

The seahorse has a head that looks like a horse, but it is soft. The seahorse can be brown, gray, or tan. When a seahorse swims by bright plants or sea things, it changes colors. A seahorse does this to stay safe. It helps the seahorse to hide from other animals.

A seahorse has bony rings and a layer of skin that feels prickly. It has a long tail, and it uses its tail to hang on to plants and weeds.

A seahorse has a long nose that is called a snout. It sucks up animals that are swimming by.

The father seahorse has a pouch in the front of his body. It is like a big pocket. The mother seahorse puts eggs inside. The babies stay there until they hatch. Baby seahorses pop out and swim away.

These fish swim in warm ocean waters. Keep watching. You might catch your own one day!

STORY QUESTIONS

1. What statement is **TRUE**?
   a. Seahorses live on farms.   c. Seahorses live on the sand.
   b. Seahorses live in lakes.   d. Seahorses live in the ocean.

2. In this passage, what does the word *prickly* mean?
   a. pointy   c. tiny
   b. shiny   d. soft

3. The author is writing this to . . .
   a. to tell you stories about a pet seahorse.
   b. to tell you things that are funny about seahorses.
   c. to make you want to buy a seahorse.
   d. to tell you facts about seahorses.

DAILY Warm-Up 17

Name _____   Date _____

OSTRICH

Did you know that the ostrich is the biggest bird in the world? Did you know it has feathers? <u>Did you know it can't fly?</u> It cannot fly, but it can run fast—very fast. It uses its wings to flap up and down and keep it cool.

It is easy to tell if ostriches are boys or girls. Girls have brown and gray feathers. Boys have black feathers. They also have white feathers.

A male ostrich has one "main hen." He digs a nest for her, and she lays the eggs in it. They both take turns sitting on the eggs to keep them warm. He also has other hens, but only has a nest with one.

When the eggs are six weeks old, they hatch, and baby chicks are born. These babies have spotted necks, and their bodies are brown and gray. They look like fluffy fur balls. Their necks are long and so are their legs. The first day they can walk and get their own food.

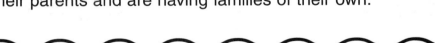

By the time they are one year old, they are as tall as their parents and are having families of their own.

STORY QUESTIONS

1. What is the biggest bird in the world?
a. ostrich
b. robin
c. bluebird
d. parrot

2. Which sentence is **NOT TRUE**?
a. When it is one year old, an ostrich is as tall as its mom and dad.
b. Ostrich babies look like fur balls.
c. Ostrich eggs hatch when they are ten weeks old.
d. Ostrich babies have spotted necks.

3. Tell what kind of sentence this is: <u>Did you know it can't fly?</u>
a. declarative
b. interrogative
c. exclamatory

DAILY Warm-Up 18

HUMMINGBIRDS

Have you ever seen the tiny bird that never stops flying? Do you know its name? Have you seen how its wings flap so fast? Have you heard a bird humming?

It is called a hummingbird. It is one of the smallest birds. It is shorter than a pack of gum. Its long bill helps it drink the juice out of flowers. The juice is called nectar.

Hummingbirds have tongues to catch insects. Their tongues are sticky. Flying makes them very hungry. That is why they are always looking for flowers. They are always drinking nectar.

They live in forests, deserts, parks, and in the mountains. They live in fields and in valleys. Hummingbirds build nests for their babies anywhere they can find a quiet spot. They hunt for bugs and juice. The mother brings the food back to feed the babies.

If you see a bird that is flying <u>quickly</u> and is very tiny, it might be a hummingbird! Keep watching!

STORY QUESTIONS

1. A **synonym** is a word that means the same thing. *Quickly* means . . .
   a. hunt.
   b. slow.
   c. fast.
   d. quiet.

2. Where do hummingbirds live?
   a. forests, deserts, and parks
   b. lakes and rivers
   c. oceans
   d. in tall trees

3. What is the name for the juice in the flower?
   a. juice
   b. nectar
   c. sticky
   d. hungry

GEORGE WASHINGTON

George Washington was the first president of the United States. He was a great man, because he gave our country a good start.

George was born in 1732. George liked to do math. His father died when he was 11, and he had to help his mother take care of the land. George had to do many chores. He grew to six feet two inches tall.

England was telling the colonies what to do and how to act. George did not like that. He became a general in the army, and he made his own uniform.

The colonies went to war, and it was very hard. The men wanted to go home. They had no money for their families. They had rags for clothes, and some of them had shoes that were falling apart. It was cold, and there was snow. They were almost out of food. The men had to fight and not get paid. George said that if they did not get paid, he would not get paid either. The soldiers stayed, and they fought as hard as they could. They won the war.

The people wanted George to be the new king. He wanted to be president. <u>They all voted for him.</u> He loved the people, and the people loved him back. He listened to them. He picked good men to work for him, and they tried to make good choices.

He wanted to do his best. He was the president for eight years. He did not live in the White House, because it was not built yet. The people wanted him to stay, and he said, "No." George wanted to go home to live with Martha. He wanted to stop working. It was time to rest.

STORY QUESTIONS

1. How did the people feel about George?

a. They all loved him.

b. They did not like him.

c. They said he was too fat.

d. They said he was happy.

2. Tell what kind of sentence this is: <u>They all voted for him.</u>

a. exclamatory

b. interrogative

c. declarative

3. When the soldiers did not get paid, what did George say he would do?

a. He would go home.

b. He would work for free, too.

c. He wanted to go out for ice cream.

DAILY Warm-Up 2 Name _____ Date _____

BETSY ROSS

When Betsy was 21, she ran away because she wanted to marry John Ross. They moved to Philadelphia. Betsy made clothes and furniture. She had a shop in the city. John was in the army.

Betsy was a friend of George Washington. She sewed buttons on his coats. She went to his home for dinner. She sat next to him in church. They talked and talked. They both wanted to be free from the English. England and the colonies went to war. George was in charge of the army.

The army won, and the people wanted a flag. It is said that Betsy was asked to make it. George Washington wanted it to have one star for each colony. He wanted the stars to have six points. She said she would make the flag, but the stars had to have five points. She worked hard to make the flag. It was red, white, and blue. It had red and white stripes. She made a flag with 13 stars. Each star was for one colony.

Whether she made the first flag or not, Betsy Ross was an important woman in history.

STORY QUESTIONS

1. If you wanted to make the flag again, what would you do?
   a. return it   c. repair it
   b. remake it   d. rebake it

2. We know Betsy because . . .
   a. she sat by George in church.
   b. she sewed buttons on coats.
   c. she ate dinner with George.
   d. it is said that she made the first flag.

3. Why did Betsy run away from home?
   a. She wanted to get a new house.
   b. She wanted to sew.
   c. She wanted to marry John Ross.

DAILY Warm-Up 3

Name _____   Date _____

THOMAS JEFFERSON

Did all presidents have to be good speakers? No, they did not. Thomas Jefferson was not good at talking. He did not like speaking in front of a lot of people. He was afraid to speak in front of a crowd. Though he did not speak well, he could write words on paper very well. That is what he did best of all.

Tom was very tall. He had freckles and sandy-colored hair. He was born on April 13, 1743. Tom loved to be out in the woods. He loved to read books. Tom went to private school.

He went to William and Mary College. He went to <u>learn</u> math and science. He went to learn to write and know the laws.

Tom became a lawyer in 1767. He wrote the Declaration of Independence. It said we would be free from England. We would make our own choices.

He was the third president. It was very hard to make the people happy. He tried very hard. There were problems with France. Some of his ideas were good. Others were bad.

After eight years, he went home and did what he wanted to do.

STORY QUESTIONS

1. What did Thomas Jefferson write?
   a. stories for his children
   b. the Declaration of Independence
   c. letters to his wife
   d. notes in his school classes

2. A **synonym** is a word that means the same thing. *Learn* means . . .
   a. study.   c. happy.
   b. free.   d. wrote.

3. What did Thomas have problems doing?
   a. asking for help
   b. writing notes in school
   c. talking in front of people

Name _____ Date _____

DOLLEY MADISON

Dolley Madison was born in 1731. She had two children, but one day her husband died. Dolley had many friends. One day her friend had her meet James Madison. He was 17 years older than Dolley. He asked her to be his wife, and she said, "Yes." It was a happy day for Dolley and James.

James Madison ran for president, and he <u>won the race</u>. They moved into the White House, and Dolley became the new first lady. She knew just what to do. She made the White House a happy place. That was her job. Dolley was always kind, and people liked her very much. Every week she gave parties. She made things look nice. She got new dishes. Dolley painted the walls. Things looked great. James and Dolley worked hard to make things happen.

One day a war came. Dolley would not leave. The White House was on fire, and smoke was in the air. The chairs were on fire, and the walls were burning. She saw the painting of George Washington on the wall. She <u>grabbed</u> it and ran. The painting was saved. James was so proud of her!

Dolley Madison was a hero. She was very brave.

STORY QUESTIONS

1. How much older was James than Dolley?
   a. 10 years
   b. 2 years
   c. 7 years
   d. 17 years

2. In the passage, "won the race" means. . .
   a. James ran the fastest of all.   c. James got a ribbon.
   b. James got to be the president.   d. James won a medal.

3. A **synonym** is a word that means the same thing. *Grabbed* means . . .
   a. took hold of
   b. let go
   c. ran after

Name _____ **Date** _____

ALBERT EINSTEIN

Have you ever wanted to know answers to things? For example, how do things work? What makes them work? Why do they work? Albert Einstein had this curiosity. He just wanted to know.

He was born in 1879 in Germany. Albert did not like to talk. He just wanted to think. He loved to build houses out of cards. It would take him a long time. He did the job slowly, because the cards had to be just right.

Albert <u>loved</u> science and was very good at it. He kept looking for why things did what they did. He found out how they worked. Albert worked on making a bomb in Germany. He worked hard to know how it worked.

In 1933 he came to America. He got a job studying how things worked. He loved his job. He wrote to the president. Albert said we had to make the bomb first. The president listened. We will always think about the things he learned in science. He was a great man.

STORY QUESTIONS

1. The word *loved* is . . .
   a. future tense.
   b. present tense.
   c. past tense

2. When did Albert come to America?
   a. 1923
   b. 1933
   c. 1879
   d. 2006

3. What one thing do we know about Albert?
   a. He loved his cat.
   b. He was the president.
   c. He was born in America.
   d. He always asked questions.

DAILY Warm-Up 6

Name _____ Date _____

GEORGE W. BUSH

George W. Bush is the 43rd president of the United States. This is his second term being president.

He was born on July 6, 1946. His family moved to Texas after he was born. He went to college, and he met Laura. She was a teacher at a school. She worked in a library. He thought she was very pretty. He wanted to ask her to be his wife, and she said, "Yes." They have two girls. Their names are Jenna and Barbara. They are grown up.

Now George Bush lives in the White House. His wife lives there, too. He and Laura have two dogs. One is Barney, and the other is Miss Beazley. They also have one cat. His name is Willie.

George likes to go to his ranch in Texas. He likes to cook for the people who work for him. He knows all their names. George likes to take walks on his ranch or ride in his truck. He likes to spend time with Laura.

It is a <u>hard</u> job to be the president. There are many things to do. There are many choices he has to make every day. Good luck, Mr. President!

STORY QUESTIONS

1. How many dogs does George Bush have?
   a. 1   c. 3
   b. 5   d. 2

2. To whom is George Bush married?
   a. Miss Beazley
   b. Jenna
   c. Laura
   d. Barney

3. Antonyms are words that mean the opposite. An antonym for *hard* is . . .
   a. tough.   c. stiff.
   b. easy.   d. solid.

MICHELLE KWAN

Do you know Michelle Kwan? She is a skater. Michelle is a great skater. She has won 42 times. No other skater has so won so many times. She has many ribbons in her house. Her mom and dad are very happy. She is happy, too.

Michelle started to skate when she was five. She won her first time when she was seven. She loved to skate. All she wanted to do was skate. She learned to turn circles on the ice. She learned to jump high in the air. She hopped up and down. It was fun for her. Day after day, she wanted to be on the ice. She loved to feel the wind in her hair.

Michelle skated many times. She kept getting better and better. Each time she won a medal. She could leap in the air, and people loved to watch her skate.

Today she is 26 years old. She has been skating for 21 years. She plans to retire and teach little boys and girls to skate.

STORY QUESTIONS

1. When we think of Michelle Kwan, we think of . . .
   a. running.
   b. skating.
   c. jumping.
   d. soccer.

2. How many times has Michelle been a winner?
   a. 24
   b. 21
   c. 42

3. A different title would be . . .
   a. "She's a Winner."
   b. "Look at Her Hit the Ball."
   c. "A New Skate."
   d. "Learning to Get on the Ice."

Name _____ **Date** _____

TIGER WOODS

Tiger is a golf star. He is from California, and he is an only child. He can hit a golf ball very far. He can hit it very well.

One day Tiger's dad cut off a big golf club. He gave it to Tiger as soon as he could walk. <u>Tiger started to hit the ball</u>. He loved to play golf with his dad. When he was three, he could play nine holes.

Now Tiger is thirty years old. He is the best golfer in the world. He has won many times. He can hit the ball <u>straight</u>. The balls go over the water. They fly over the grass. He can hit the holes.

Tiger has made a lot of money playing golf. He can thank his dad for the cutting off the golf club when he was little. It gave Tiger a great start.

STORY QUESTIONS

1. Antonyms are words that mean the opposite. An antonym for *straight* is . . .
   a. in a line.
   b. crooked.
   c. in the hole.
   d. under the bed

2. Why do you think Tiger is such a good golfer?
   a. His dad put a club in his hand when he learned to walk.
   b. He is good.
   c. He is a nice guy.
   d. He likes to golf.

3. Tell what kind of sentence this is: <u>Tiger started to hit the ball</u>.
   a. none of these   c. interrogative
   b. exclamatory   d. declarative

CONDOLEEZA RICE

They call her "Condie" for short. Her real name is very long. She was an only child. Her mother was a music teacher, and Condie's father was a preacher.

She loved to play the piano when she was little. Condie dreamed of being a pianist. She wanted to play the piano very well. She played and played. It was her dream. It was the thing she wanted most of all.

One day Condie turned 15. She knew she could not play as well as she wanted. She wanted to help make the world a better place so Condie went to college. She studied hard.

Now, she speaks five languages. She works for the White House and <u>travels</u> to places far away.

She is one of the most powerful ladies in U.S. history. Some people think she will be a good leader for the U.S. Maybe she will be the first lady to be president. No one knows, but she will work hard at what she does. She always does!

STORY QUESTIONS

1. What did Condie want to be when she grew up?
   a. a president
   b. a first lady
   c. a pianist
   d. a college teacher

2. What word best describes Condie?
   a. hard-worker
   b. lazy
   c. funny
   d. boring

3. A **synonym** is a word that means the same thing. *Travels* means . . .
   a. has a suitcase.
   b. stays in one city.
   c. goes places.

DAILY Warm-Up 10

Name _____ Date _____

WALT DISNEY

Do you like to be happy? Walt Disney did. He liked to make people laugh, and he liked them to be happy.

He was born in 1901. Walt lived on a farm with his mom and dad. He had three brothers, and he had one sister. Walt loved to draw, and he liked to take pictures.

When he was 16, he wanted to help out. He wanted to go into the army. They said, "No." He asked the Red Cross if he could help, and they said, "Yes."

After the war, Walt went to Hollywood. He had $40.00, pencils, and paper. He had nothing else.

His brother, Roy Disney, was waiting for him. They made movies. Walt made up Mickey Mouse. They made it into a movie, and people liked it. They wanted more.

Walt made others. He made *Bambi* and *Dumbo*. He made a park that was fun. There are so many things to see at the park. It has rides to make people happy. <u>Do you know what park it is?</u>

STORY QUESTIONS

1. How much money did Walt have when he got to Hollywood?
 a. $30
 b. $40
 c. $70
 d. $100

2. Which one was **NOT** something Walt liked to do?
 a. laugh
 b. draw pictures
 c. make fun of people
 d. make movies

3. Tell what kind of sentence this is: <u>Do you know what park it is?</u>
 a. none of these
 b. exclamatory
 c. declarative
 d. interrogative

DAILY Warm-Up 11

Name _____

Date _____

DENZEL WASHINGTON

Denzel is a good actor. He has made many movies. He thinks his job is very important.

He was born in 1954. His mom cut hair, and his daddy was a preacher. He had one sister and one brother. Denzel liked rules. He always tried to do his best. He did a good job in school. He worked hard. He got good grades.

He wanted to be a doctor, but it was not meant to be. At school he acted in a play, and Denzel was very good. He wanted to change his mind and become an actor.

Denzel went to Hollywood. He met Paulette in a play. He asked her to marry him, and she said, "Yes." They have two boys and two girls.

He keeps making movies. He helps his boys play sports, and he helps his girls play sports. He loves his wife's cooking.

Denzel tries hard to be a good dad. He tries to love his wife, and he does his best in movies. Denzel is loved by many people.

STORY QUESTIONS

1. What do the words "change his mind" mean?
   a. He wanted to do something different.
   b. He got a new mind.
   c. He wanted to go to a new place.
   d. He wanted to play a new game.

2. Which is **NOT** a fact about Denzel?
   a. He is a great actor.
   b. He has seven children.
   c. His wife is named Paulette.

3. **Homophones** are words that sound the same, but are spelled differently. Which homophone is used correctly?
   a. I saw the <u>be</u> sit by me.
   b. Will you <u>bee</u> my friend?
   c. She will <u>bee</u> cooking his lunch.
   d. Denzel will <u>be</u> in more movies.

DAILY Warm-Up 12

Name _____ Date _____

SANDRA BULLOCK

Sandra Bullock is an actress. Many people like to see her act. They go to her movies. She is funny, and she has a snort for a laugh. Sandra is very different from the other actors and actresses.

She was born on July 26, 1964. Her dad was a scientist. Her mom was a clerk at her dad's office.

Sandra was a busy girl. She liked to know how things worked and liked to explore them her way. One day her mom told her not to touch a light bulb. Sandra hit it very hard. It broke. She got a big cut, and they had to take her to the doctor.

In school kids called her ugly. They did not like her hair, and they did not like her clothes. Sandra said, <u>"I will not be like that!"</u> She did not want others to get hurt like she did. Sandra wanted to be a movie star.

Today she has made a lot of movies. She kept going and did not give up. If it was hard, she worked harder. People all over the world like to watch the parts she plays. Sandra still has one rule, "Be nice to all people you meet!"

STORY QUESTIONS

1. Why does Sandra think it is good to be nice to everyone?
   a. She knows what it feels like to have people laugh at you.
   b. She wants to make a face.
   c. She thinks making fun of other kids is fun.

2. Why did Sandra break the light bulb?
   a. She wanted to turn it on.
   b. She wanted to know how it worked.
   c. She wanted to jump a fence.
   d. Her mother told her to do it.

3. Tell what kind of sentence this is: <u>I would not be like that!</u>
   a. none of these   c. interrogative
   b. declarative   d. exclamatory

DAILY Warm-Up 13

Name _____   Date _____

BRUCE WILLIS

Do you know who Bruce Willis is? Most of the world does. He is a movie star. Bruce can play many kinds of people. He can be funny, or he can make you cry. His <u>acting</u> is one of the best.

Bruce is not his real first name. His real name is Walter. He was born in March 19, 1955. His dad was in the army. He was born in Germany. His dad moved the family to the U.S. when Walter was two years old.

Walter had many friends. He was funny, and he worked very hard. Walter was a wrestler in high school. He wanted to be a movie star.

One day he came to California. He tried out, but he did not get the part. He tried out again and got the job. He then changed his name to Bruce. Bruce has made many movies. He still loves to act.

STORY QUESTIONS

1. Synonyms are words that mean the same thing. *Acting* is another word for . . .
   a. writing a book.
   b. riding a bike.
   c. pretending to be someone else for a movie or a play.
   d. eating a lollipop.

2. What is Bruce's real first name?
   a. Walter
   b. Bruce
   c. Fred
   d. Dave

3. What can we guess Bruce will do?
   a. He will stop making movies.
   b. He will keep making movies.
   c. He will write kids' books.

DAILY Warm-Up 14

Name _____

Date _____

LAURA BUSH

Laura Bush is the first Lady. <u>She was born in 1946.</u> Laura has two girls. She is married to George W. Bush. He is the 43rd president of the United States.

She lives in the White House and works very hard. Laura has many jobs. She helps kids in schools by talking to them. She tells them that it is good to learn to read.

She tells them they should say "no" to drugs. She thinks all kids should have someone who cares about them in their lives.

Laura also works hard with teachers. She tells them to be <u>kind</u> to others. She wants others to work hard to make the world a better place, too.

We can learn to help others, and we can learn to show kindness by acting like the First Lady, Laura Bush.

STORY QUESTIONS

1. Antonyms are words that mean the opposite. *Kind* is an antonym for . . .
   a. nice
   b. mean
   c. kind
   d. happy

2. Laura Bush has two . . .
   a. cats.
   b. horses.
   c. girls.
   d. chicks.

3. Tell what kind of sentence this is: <u>She was born in 1946.</u>
   a. declarative
   b. exclamatory
   c. interrogative

DAILY Warm-Up 15 Name _____ Date _____

BABE RUTH

Even though Babe Ruth was born many years ago, in 1895, you may know something about him. His full name was George Herman Ruth. When he was a child, Babe's mother and father could not care for him, so they sent him to a place with other children—an orphanage. As a child, Babe had to work very hard. He had to do many chores, and he had to go to school at the same time.

Babe liked to play ball. He was on the school team, and he became the best hitter. He was also the best pitcher.

When he grew up, Babe became a baseball player. He was on three teams. He played for the Red Sox, Yankees, and Braves. His coach called him "Babe."

Babe hit 60 home runs in one year. It was the most home runs until 1961. He is in the Baseball Hall of Fame. Babe Ruth was a great ballplayer!

STORY QUESTIONS

1. What place did Babe's parents send him to?
   a. a park
   b. a camp
   c. an orphanage
   d. a store

2. From this passage, we can guess that . . .
   a. Babe was a bad boy.
   b. the thing that Babe did best was play baseball.
   c. Babe was not a hard worker.
   d. Babe was a girl.

3. Which **compound** word means "a game played with a ball and bases"?
   a. soccer
   b. baseball
   c. basketball

Name _____   Date _____

HANK AARON

Hank Aaron hit more home runs than anyone. Hank hit 755 home runs in his time playing baseball. He broke Babe Ruth's record. It was a great day for Hank.

He was born in 1934. Hank loved to play baseball and always had a bat in his hands. He played out in the field. He could catch the ball, and he could hit the ball. Each year he got better and better.

When Hank was in high school, the Black Bears wanted him to play for them. He told them he would play. He could hit a ball very hard.

When Hank grew up, he played for the Braves and the Brewers. Hank hit home runs every year.

Many <u>fans</u> were happy, and they cheered for Hank. Other people became mad at him. Hank Aaron was not white, so they did not think he should be able to hit so well. They did not think he should be able to break a white man's record for hitting the ball.

When it was over, it did not matter. Hank was a great ballplayer. He did his job, and he did it well.

STORY QUESTIONS

1. Why didn't some people like Hank Aaron?
- a. He was not white.
- b. He could not hit a ball.
- c. He was a slow runner.
- d. He had a bad name.

2. "Fans" are . . .
- a. people who move up and down.
- b. people who come to a game to watch players.
- c. people who are in boxes.
- d. people who like milk.

3. How many home runs did Hank hit in all?
- a. 1934
- b. 755
- c. 557
- d. 102

DAILY
Warm-Up 17

Name _____ Date _____

CHRISTOPHER COLUMBUS

Christopher Columbus was a sailor. He lived on the seas. He worked for the queen of Spain. She wanted him to find places that no one knew about. He tried to find ways to get things from place to place by using the water. The queen gave him money to sail his ships. She paid him to find new places. He loved to sail. He loved to study maps.

Life on the sea was hard. Christopher was the captain. Only a few men had rooms to sleep in. The rest had to sleep outside on the decks. It was very cold, and the ship moved a lot.

The water came over the edges of the boat. The sailors sang to pass the time. They did chores. They cleaned the deck, and they prayed. The water went on and on.

Christopher found new places. He found bananas and coffee. He found rice. Christopher shared corn and potatoes with the people he met, and they traded.

Most of all, he loved to be on the water looking for new places.

STORY QUESTIONS

1. What was Christopher?
   a. a doctor   c. a sailor
   b. a farmer   d. a teacher

2. What **compound** word from the text means "to be out in the weather"?
   a. outfit
   b. outcome
   c. outdo
   d. outside

3. Christopher spent most of his life living on . . .
   a. Mars.
   b. land.
   c. water.

DAILY Warm-Up 18 Name _____ Date _____

HARRIET TUBMAN

<u>One lady did great things!</u> Her real name was Araminta. People know her as Harriet Tubman. Others called her Moses.

She was born a slave in 1820. Life was hard for her. It was hard for her family. They had to work long hours. They had to pick cotton. Their house was a shack. It was very cold in the winter and very hot in the summer.

When she was a teen, she ran away. They did not catch her. She ran to the North. There were no slaves up there. People did not care about the color of your skin.

She got a job working for the army. She was a nurse. She was a soldier, and she was a scout.

Harriet also helped other slaves get away from the South. She ran the Underground Railroad. It was not a train. She was the conductor, but she did not have a train.

She helped <u>runaways</u>. She helped them find places to hide. Other people helped her. They gave the slaves food. She led them north to the land where they could be free.

Harriet was a hero. She was brave and she helped others.

STORY QUESTIONS

1. What did Harriet do to make the world better?
   a. She was mean to people.
   b. She cleaned houses.
   c. She helped slaves escape.
   d. She made cookies.

2. "Runaways" are . . .
   a. a place to land a plane.
   b. a candy bar.
   c. rabbits.
   d. people who run away

3. Tell what kind of sentence this is: <u>One lady did great things!</u>
   a. interrogative
   b. exclamatory
   c. declarative

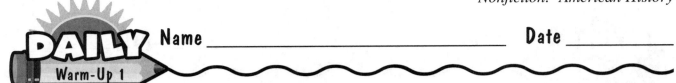

Name _____ Date _____

AIRPLANE

Two men made the first airplane that worked. They were brothers. Their names were Orville and Wilber Wright. The airplane was made of wood and was called a "flyer."

Before the brothers invented the first airplane, Orville and Wilber opened a bike shop. They fixed bikes when things went wrong. They also made their own bikes. They saved the money they made.

The men used the money to build things that could fly. The first two things did not work. The third "flyer" did. It stayed in the air for 12 seconds. It went 120 feet. It was the start of a great invention!

Orville and Wilber made other planes. The planes got better and faster. Now their first plane is in a museum for the world to see.

STORY QUESTIONS

1. How did the brothers make money to build a plane?
   a. They picked up trash.
   b. The made cars.
   c. They made and sold bikes.
   d. They got it from the bank.

2. Why do you think they called the first plane a "flyer"?
   a. It was a bird.
   b. It looked funny.
   c. They liked the name.
   d. It could go up in the air.

3. How did the men know each other?
   a. They were brothers.
   b. They were best friends.
   c. They met at school.

DAILY Warm-Up 2

Name _____ Date _____

CELL PHONES

Did you know the idea of cell phones is only about 40 years old? It was made in the 1960s.

The first cell phone that was for sale was in Japan. They made it in 1979. Cell phones became available for sale in the U.S. in 1983.

At first, cell phone calls were hard to make. Only a few people in one place could talk at the same time. They were big and heavy. Many times the calls would end, and the call was lost.

Today most families have one cell phone. Some have more than one. They are very light. Many of them can take pictures. Kids can play games. They are fast. Cell phones are little. They can be green, red, or blue. They can be any color you want.

Today you can use them to call almost anywhere. We can talk to people all over the world.

STORY QUESTIONS

1. When did they first think of cell phones?
   a. 1940s
   b. 1960s
   c. 1990s
   d. 1920s

2. Which is **NOT** a fact about today's cell phone?
   a. They have games.
   b. They are small.
   c. They are big and heavy.
   d. Most families have more than one cell phone.

3. Which **compound** word means "the day we are in"?
   a. today
   b. Sunday
   c. Monday

DAILY Warm-Up 3

Name _____ Date _____

COKE

Do you like Coke®? Most people do. It is a soft drink that looks like syrup. It is brown and sweet. It can be in a can, or it can be in a glass. It can be in a tall thin bottle.

It was invented on May 8, 1886. The man who made it was John Pemberton. He was a man who made medicine for sick people. He was also an inventor.

John made many kinds of syrup. He made pills and syrups to make people feel better. He sold them in a store.

John also made a drink that people liked to sip for fun. It was made out of wine, coffee beans, and caffeine. People all over wanted his drink.

One day a new law was made. No one could use wine. No one could drink it.

John still wanted to make money. He still wanted to sell his drinks, but they could not have wine in the drink. He put sugar and fruit in the mix. It looked good, and it had a good taste. People loved it. It was called Coca-Cola®.

John made the drink we have today.

STORY QUESTIONS

1. What does Coke look like?
   a. bread
   b. pancakes
   c. oil
   d. syrup

2. When did John make the first Coke?
   a. 1886
   b. 2006
   c. 1885
   d. 1826

3. The author wrote this to tell you about . . .
   a. how to climb trees.
   b. how to add sugar to syrup.
   c. how we got Coke.

DAILY Warm-Up 4

Name _____   Date _____

THE IRON

Have you ever tried to help your mom iron? It is hot. You have to be careful not to burn yourself.

The first iron was made in 1882. Henry Seeley made it. He lived in New York. He called it a "flat iron." It was big and black. You had to be strong to use it. It did not have a cord.

The iron was 15 pounds, and it was hard to pick up. It took a long time to get hot. It had to be put on the fire.

Today, irons are very light. They go in the wall with a plug. It has a long cord, and it makes the iron get hot very fast. You do not have to wait for a long time.

Irons make clothes look nice. They have changed and gotten better. Aren't you glad we have the new irons?

STORY QUESTIONS

1. For what can you use an iron?
  a. to fix a bike
  b. to start the car
  c. to get out the wrinkles out of things
  d. to read

2. The first iron was called a . . .
  a. "flat iron."
  b. "round iron."
  c. "sandwich."
  d. "hot thing."

3. Who made the first iron?
  a. Harriet Tubman   c. George Bush
  b. Hank Aaron   d. Henry Seeley

DAILY Warm-Up 5 Name _____ Date _____

THE POPSICLE

Do you love Popsicles®? Most kids do. Did you know that a little boy made the first one? He was only 11 years old. His name was Frank. Frank lived in San Francisco.

One night in 1905, Frank forgot to put his fruit drink away. He left the drink outside. He left a stirring stick in it. He went to bed. That night it got very cold. The fruit juice froze. The stick was still in the middle of the juice, and it got stuck.

In the morning, Frank found his fruit juice. It was frozen. The stick was stuck in the middle. He took a bite, and it was good. It was great! Frank made more and more kinds. He froze fudge. He froze other drinks. They were all good.

Frank's mistake turned into a big frozen deal!

STORY QUESTIONS

1. Frank made the first Popsicle . . .
   a. for a snack.
   b. on purpose.
   c. by mistake.
   d. for a joke.

2. Where did Frank live?
   a. San Francisco
   b. Minnesota
   c. Kansas
   d. Texas

3. Why did Frank's juice freeze over night?
   a. It was in the freezer.
   b. It was very cold at night.
   c. It was in the snow.

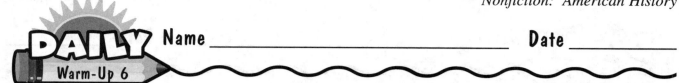

Name _____ Date _____

LIGHT BULBS

Do you have light bulbs all over your house? Most people do. Light bulbs help us see better in the day. They help us see better at night. We can thank Thomas Edison.

He made a bulb that had light inside. It could glow for 1,500 hours. It could be put in homes. It could be placed in churches. It could be in the jails. It can work in the park. The bulb showed light when it was dark. It made rooms brighter than before.

It took him a long time to make the light bulb. He had to try many different things. When the job was <u>done</u>, he had a good light bulb. People were able to get more done in their day. Their eyes did not get as sore. It was easier to see what you were doing.

Life is easier. We can see well. Thank you, Thomas!

STORY QUESTIONS

1. Why do we use light bulbs?
    a. to help us make friends
    b. to help us eat pizza
    c. to help us see better
    d. to help us go to the zoo

2. Synonyms are words that mean the same thing. The word *done* can be a synonym for . . .
    a. ended.   c. happy.
    b. started.   d. going to happen.

3. Where don't you find light bulbs?
    a. in a house
    b. in the ocean
    c. in a library

DAILY Warm-Up 7 Name _____ Date _____

KOOL-AID

When it is hot, does your mother mix Kool-Aid®? Many mothers make it on hot sunny days. Kids like to make it, too.

Edwin Perkins made Kool-Aid in 1927. He had a company that sold perfume and cards. After a while, he wanted to sell more things. So, he tried to make things no one else had thought of.

First, he made a drink called "Fruit Smack." He sold it in little glass bottles. People liked the drink. He changed the name to "Kool-Ade." He did not put it in bottles. It was dry. He put it in little packets, and people went crazy over it.

Edwin changed the name again. He called it "Kool-Aid." This time the name was a good name. He made it in cherry, grape, and orange. He made other flavors, too.

The new name was great. The drink was great. Moms just had to add sugar. They just had to mix it up with water. Kids today still like Kool-Aid on a hot day!

STORY QUESTIONS

1. "Fruit Smack" was . . .
   a. getting hit with a "fruit" punch in the arm.
   b. something to put on your lips.
   c. a fruit cup.
   d. the first name for Kool-Aid.

2. Which man made the first Kool-Aid?
   a. Edwin Perkins
   b. Laura Bush
   c. Babe Ruth
   d. Denzel Washington

3. In the passage, Kool-Aid was for making kids . . .
   a. hot on a cool day.
   b. cool on a hot day.
   c. feel strong.

MARSHMALLOWS

Did you know that there was candy 2,000 years ago? It was made in Egypt. It was marshmallow candy. This candy was made from a root of a plant.

It was made out of the mallow root. This plant grew in the swamps. It grew in places that had lots of weeds. It was white inside. It was <u>sticky</u> and sweet.

Today we still eat candy that is made out of marshmallows. It is white and sweet. It is not made out of the root anymore. The candy is made out of gelatin. It still tastes good. It is still sticky and white.

As long as there are children, there will always be candy made out of sweet things.

STORY QUESTIONS

1. What did they use to make the first marshmallow candy?
   a. a store
   b. a bush
   c. a tree
   d. a root

2. The word *sticky* means . . .
   a. messy and gooey.
   b. clean and neat.
   c. spotless.
   d. dirt-free.

3. Today they do not use the root to make the candy. What do they use?
   a. gelatin
   b. gum
   c. sugar

DAILY Warm-Up 9

Name _____ Date _____

MICROWAVE OVEN

Do you think mistakes are good? Some mistakes are. One man made a mistake that is good for all of us.

One day a man was working in a lab. His name was Percy Spencer. He had a candy bar in his pocket. He was studying tubes. The tubes were vacuum tubes. He was studying microwaves in the tubes.

The chocolate bar melted, and it got all over in his pocket. The microwaves in the tubes had made the candy melt.

Percy started to think and think. He worked with the waves. He tried many things. They all worked. These microwaves cooked food faster than an oven.

I am glad his candy bar melted in his pocket that day. Now, we can all use the microwave oven. It can cook our food fast!

STORY QUESTIONS

1. What melted in Percy's pocket?
   a. his crayon
   b. his soup
   c. a chocolate bar
   d. his ice

2. What idea did Percy get?
   a. to make a machine that cooks food very fast
   b. to make more messes
   c. to buy more candy bars
   d. to buy new pants

3. What do we call Percy's machine?
   a. toaster
   b. microwave
   c. oven

Name _____   Date _____

Q-TIPS

On a sunny morning a mother wanted to clean her baby's ears. She thought and thought. She found a toothpick, and then she got a piece of cotton.

This mother put the cotton on the end of the toothpick. She put it in the baby's ear. It worked! The baby had clean ears.

Do you know what this mother made? She made a Q-tip®. She told her husband. His name was Leo. Leo liked the idea. He took a stick made out of wood, and he put cotton on each end. He called them Baby Gays.

Today we can buy them in the store. They are made out of white cardboard and cotton. The name has changed to Q-tips. We use them to clean small things. We use them for glue. We use them to spread paint. We use them for many things. And, we still use them to clean ears.

STORY QUESTIONS

1. The first Q-tip was made out of . . .
   a. a straw and a brick.
   b. a toothpick and a piece of cotton.
   c. a stick and a stone.
   d. a box and a rock.

2. What could be a different title for this passage?
   a. "A Baby's First Day"
   b. "Rolling with the Baby"
   c. "Cleaner Ears"
   d. "My White Cotton"

3. Today, Q-tips can be used to . . .
   a. do many things.
   b. only for cleaning ears.
   c. only for gluing things.

DAILY Name _____ Date _____

Warm-Up 11

SEWING MACHINE

A long time ago people had to sew clothes by hand. <u>They had to make pants by hand.</u> They had to make shoes by hand. There were no machines to make the work go faster.

In 1830, a man had an idea. His name was Barthelemy. He lived in France. He wanted to make a machine that could sew faster than a person could sew by hand.

He made one that would work. It had a needle and thread that went up and down. The cloth stayed together. He could make clothes faster.

Other people who made clothes were angry. They burned his shop to the ground. They did not like it that he made a new machine. They were scared he would make all the money.

Two men made new machines. Elias Howe made a machine. Isaac Singer made a machine. They all could sew. Isaac's was the best. It is still a great sewing machine today. It is called the Singer® Sewing machine.

STORY QUESTIONS

1. How has sewing changed?
  a. Today we sew by hand. All of the machines do not work.
  b. Today we sew with machines. They used to sew by hand.
  c. We sew with machines. They all sewed with machines.
  d. Today we do not sew at all. They did not sew.

2. Which sentence is **FALSE**?
  a. Elias made the best sewing machine.
  b. The Singer machine was made by Isaac Singer.
  c. Sewing machines made sewing go faster.
  d. Barthelemy made the first sewing machine.

3. Tell what kind of sentence this is: <u>They had to make pants by hand.</u>
  a. none of these   c. interrogative
  b. exclamatory   d. declarative

DAILY
Warm-Up 12

Name _____

Date _____

UMBRELLAS

Umbrellas were made a long time ago. They were made for keeping the sun out of your eyes. They were made for keeping cool on <u>hot</u> days.

In China, they made the first umbrella to use in the rain. They put wax and paint on it. This made the rain run off the sides. It kept them dry when they walked. It kept them dry in the storm. They used bones from whales, and they used wood from the trees.

In 1852, Samuel Fox made a new kind of umbrella. It had steel parts. It had soft cloth. It was easy to put up and easy to put down. It was very light to carry.

Today umbrellas come in all sizes and shapes. They come in all colors. Some people use them in the rain. Others use them when it is hot. Some have umbrellas just for fun.

Today, umbrellas have many uses!

STORY QUESTIONS

1. For what was the first umbrella used?
   a. keeping cool on hot days
   b. keeping hot on cools days
   c. catching the rain
   d. keeping the person dry

2. If I wanted an umbrella, the best one to buy would be one that . . .
   a. was too big to carry.
   b. had large holes.
   c. was any shape or color.
   d. was very heavy.

3. Antonyms are words that mean the opposite. *Hot* is an antonym for . . .
   a. lukewarm.   c. warm.
   b. sunny.   d. cold.

DAILY Name _____ Date _____
Warm-Up 13

WIPERS

Mary Anderson had a great idea. She saw that streetcars had a hard time running in the rain. The windows got all runny with water. It was hard to see outside, and it was hard to drive down the street. It was not safe for the riders on rainy days.

She thought and thought. Mary had a good idea. She made wipers that could work on the outside of the car. They had a button inside the streetcar to push in the rain. She hoped it would work.

When it rained, the driver pressed the button. The wipers went back and forth. They took the rain off the window. It made it easier to drive down the street. It made the people inside feel safer, and the driver could see where he was going.

Mary's idea worked. People liked the wipers. They put them on cars, and they worked, too. Her idea went all over the world.

STORY QUESTIONS

1. Mary got the idea for wipers because . . .
   a. she liked to help others.
   b. rain made her happy.
   c. she liked the rain.
   d. street cars had a hard time working in the rain.

2. Where is the one place you will not find wipers today?
   a. on a bank   c. on a bus
   b. on a car   d. on a truck

3. How do wipers help drivers?
   a. They can see better in the rain.
   b. They can drive faster in the snow.
   c. They can talk louder.
   d. They can watch the wipers move up and down.

BAND-AIDS

Earle Dickson was a man who bought cotton. He had a big job. He traveled to many places to work. He worked for a big company.

His wife liked to cook. She cut herself many times. Earle was getting <u>tired</u> of her cutting her fingers when he was not home. He had an idea.

Earle made a small, thin strip. He made it so that it was easy to put on a cut. It was small. It was sterile and did not have germs. If he was not home, his wife could put it on by herself.

She liked the strips. They stayed on her fingers, and they were easy to use. She could put them on by herself.

Earl told his boss. His boss liked the strips, too. They called them Band-Aids®. In 1920, they sold them to the public. People all over liked them, too. They worked. They came in many sizes. <u>Band-Aids were born!</u>

STORY QUESTIONS

1. Why did Earle make Band-Aids?
  a. He didn't like blood.
  b. He was in the car most of the time.
  c. His wife kept cutting her fingers.
  d. He had a lot of money.

2. "Band-Aids were born!" means that . . .
  a. Earle had a good idea. Other people could use his idea, too.
  b. They were born at the hospital.
  c. Band Aids is the name of a boy.
  d. None of these.

3. A **synonym** is a word that means the same thing. *Tired* is another word for . . .
  a. jumpy.   c. sad.
  b. worn out.   d. happy.

DAILY Name _____ Date _____
Warm-Up 15

BASKETBALL

Many years ago, there was not a lot to do in the winter. It was icy, and the students could not play much in the cold.

James Naismith was a teacher in Canada. He taught gym class. He wanted to keep playing games in the winter.

He took a soccer ball on a cold morning. He put two wooden baskets at the ends of the gym. He told the players to try and get the ball into the baskets. They ran up and down with the ball. They tried to get it in the wooden basket.

James made up new baskets in the air. The players liked the ones in the air better. They told their friends. These friends told others. Soon people all over the world were playing this new game. They were using a ball that could bounce. They were trying to get it in the basket.

Today, we play when it is cold and when it is hot. We play inside or outside. Basketball is played all over the world. James, you were a genius!

STORY QUESTIONS

1. James was a . . .
   a. doctor.
   b. teacher.
   c. nurse.
   d. worker.

2. What words best describe James?
   a. not fun at all
   b. boring
   c. likes to think of new things
   d. just likes to sit and watch TV

3. Where do people play basketball today?
   a. all over the world
   b. in trees
   c. in the snow
   d. under a rock

DAILY Warm-Up 16 Name _____ Date _____

THE TELEPHONE

In the 1800s, people had to wait a long time to get news from other places. It had to come by letters. <u>It had to come by horse.</u> Or, people had to tell others the news. It was hard to find out what was going on in the world.

Alexander Graham Bell changed that. He dreamed and dreamed. He wanted people in faraway places to talk to each other. He wanted them to know what was going on.

He took a wire and put things on both ends. He talked into one end. His friend talked into the other. They did it many times. They tried many kinds of wires. One day they could hear what the other one was saying. They could talk to each other on the wire.

The two men called this new idea the telephone. It means "far sound."

Before long, people could talk all over the country. It made them happy. They could hear news from other places. They could call to say "hello." They could call when they were happy. They did not have to have a reason to call.

The telephone made the world a smaller place.

STORY QUESTIONS

1. How did the families get news long ago?
   a. by cell phone
   b. by phone
   c. by letters or people telling it to them
   d. by computer

2. Which words best tell us about the phone?
   a. It makes getting news easier and faster.
   b. It is too big.
   c. It does not work.
   d. It is not a good invention.

3. Tell what kind of sentence this is: <u>It had to come by horse</u>.
   a. declarative   c. interrogative
   b. exclamatory   d. none of these

DAILY Warm-Up 17   Name _____   Date _____

BRAILLE

What would you do if you could not see with your eyes? Would you be able to read? Would you be able to write? Would you be able to see the world?

Yes! You would be able to read and write. You could see the world because of one brave boy.

In 1809, a boy was born in France. His name was Louis Braille. He had good eyes. He could see all the things in the world.

Before he was 13, he became blind. He could not see the trees. He could not see the birds. He could only hear the sounds.

Louis wanted to make life better for other blind people. He made up a code with dots. The dots are like bumps on a paper. Each group of dots is a letter. Others are numbers. Blind people could read words, and they could write letters. They could see the world by touching the dots on the paper.

Today people all over the world can read and write in Braille. They can see without using their eyes because of Louis!

STORY QUESTIONS

1. How did the code with dots get the name Braille?
   a. Louis Braille made it up.
   b. It sounded like a good name.
   c. It looked good on paper.

2. When Louis was a little boy, he could . . .
   a. not see. He was blind.
   b. be a fireman.
   c. see like we can see.
   d. write music and poems.

3. How did Louis help blind people so they could read and write?
   a. He was a teacher.
   b. He cut paper into circles.
   c. He ran a big race.
   d. He made raised dots to use on paper. They can make words and letters.

DAILY Name _____ Date _____
Warm-Up 18

DIAPERS

Do you have a baby at your house? Does he or she wear diapers? Can you throw them away?

In 1950, a mother named Marion had an idea. She did not like the diapers that were made out of cloth. They were too much work. They smelled bad. It took too much time to clean them. She wanted to make <u>something</u> better. Marion went to work. She tried making them out of many kinds of things. Marion made them out of plastic. She tried to sell the idea. No one said it would work. They said it would flop. They did not want to try her idea.

Marion was sure it would work. She sold them all by herself. Mothers loved her idea.

Marion made moms all over the world happy. They had more time for their babies. They had less mess to clean up. They did not have to wash diapers or let them dry. All they needed was a trashcan.

She was sure her idea was going to work. She was right!

STORY QUESTIONS

1. Why did Marion sell the diapers by herself?
   a. She needed money.
   b. She wanted to sell them.
   c. No one wanted to buy the idea.
   d. Her idea was not good.

2. Which sentence is an **opinion**?
   a. Throw-away diapers are easy to clean up.
   b. You can throw them away.
   c. Marion is the smartest lady in the world.
   d. Diapers were made in 1950.

3. Which **compound word** from the text means "one thing"?
   a. everything
   b. something
   c. nothing

DAILY Name _____ Date _____
Warm-Up 1

MAMMALS

We can look at living things, and we can put them into groups. One group is called mammals.

Mammals all have fur or hair. Their fur or hair can keep them warm. It covers some or all parts of their bodies.

Most of their babies are born alive. They are like little copies of their parents. They look just like them.

Some other mammals live on land. People are mammals. They have a lot of hair on the top of their heads. Dogs and cats are mammals. They have fur all over their bodies. Rabbits and zebras are mammals, too. They also have fur all over their bodies.

Other mammals live in the water. Whales and dolphins live in the ocean. They do not have long fur or hair. Their skin is smooth, but they are still mammals.

Some of them live in and out of the water. Sea lions do this. They have very short fur. They sit in the sun during the day. They also swim in the water much of the day and at night.

STORY QUESTIONS

1. Which sentence below is **NOT TRUE**?
   a. People are mammals.
   b. Rabbits have fur all over their bodies.
   c. Dolphins can live on land.
   d. Sea lions swim in water.

2. When a mammal has a baby, you can guess that it will . . .
   a. have wings.   c. look like its mom and dad.
   b. be inside a shell.   d. have long legs.

3. Which one is **NOT** a mammal?
   a. a pig
   b. a crow
   c. a cow

Name _____ Date _____

BIRDS

Birds are not like mammals.

First, they all have feathers. The feathers are very light. They come in many colors and sizes. Each bird has special feathers. The feathers keep them warm. Some of them help the bird to fly.

Birds do not have babies that are born alive. They lay eggs. The eggs have hard shells. Birds lay eggs in their nests. They sit on them to keep them warm. For example, the father ostrich sits on the eggs and makes sure they are warm. When they are ready, they hatch. Baby birds come out of the shells.

Some birds have feathers, but they cannot fly. The ostrich cannot fly, but it can run fast.

Birds are a different kind of animal. They are not like a mammal or a fish. They are like themselves!

STORY QUESTIONS

1. How is the ostrich different from the other birds?
   a. It cannot fly.
   b. It is not a bird.
   c. It is small.
   d. It only likes to eat bananas.

2. The author wanted you to learn about . . .
   a. animals that are mammals.
   b. animals that are birds.
   c. animals that are insects.
   d. animals that are fish.

3. What do all birds have?
   a. scales
   b. feathers
   c. whiskers

DAILY Name _____ Date _____

Warm-Up 3

FISH

Fish are another kind of animal. Fish are not like mammals. They are not like birds. Fish live in water. Most of them hatch out of eggs. They have scales on their bodies. They have gills and fins. They have a tail, eyes, and a mouth.

The scales are small shapes on their bodies. They look like pieces of paper cut into small shapes. The scales help to keep the fish safe. They give them protection.

Fish have <u>gills</u> on the sides of their bodies. These gills look like small slits. These small slits open and close. They help the fish to breathe in the water.

The fins help the fish move around in the water. They help it stay afloat in the water.

The tail moves to help the fish move fast or slowly. It makes it easy to move from place to place.

Eyes help them to see where they are going, and the mouth opens to eat smaller fish or algae.

Fish are fun to watch. They are always moving and always on the go!

STORY QUESTIONS

1. Where do all fish live?
   a. in a school
   b. in the sink
   c. in a bowl
   d. in water

2. A **gill** is a small slit on the side of a fish. What does it do?
   a. helps the fish breathe
   b. makes the fish look nice
   c. tells the fish to go up or go down

3. The author wanted you to learn about . . .
   a. animals that are mammals.
   b. animals that are fish.
   c. animals that are insects.
   d. animals that are birds.

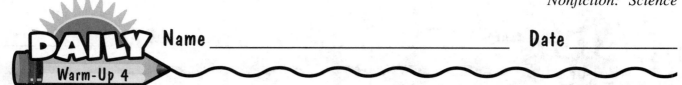

Name _____ Date _____

REPTILES

Many types of animals live in our world. Reptiles are one of these kinds. They are like fish because they lay eggs. Most of them have scales, but others have feet and tails. Some have hard shells.

All reptiles move. They can walk or crawl. A snake is the one kind of reptile that does not have legs. It can only crawl across the ground on its belly.

Lizards and turtles are reptiles. Lizards have scales on their bodies. They have legs and a long tail. They have a tongue that is split in the middle.

Turtles have a hard shell. They have a tail and four legs. When they get scared, they hide inside their shells.

Reptiles are busy. They can walk and crawl. Some can swim in the water. Life is always moving.

STORY QUESTIONS

1. How are reptiles like fish?
   a. They can walk.
   b. They lay eggs.
   c. They can crawl.
   d. They have hard shells.

2. Which one is **NOT** a reptile?
   a. lizard   c. snake
   b. turtle   d. shark

3. **Homophones** are words that sound the same, but do not mean the same thing. Which homophone is used correctly?
   a. Turtles have <u>for</u> legs.
   b. Reptiles have <u>four</u> legs.
   c. We went to the zoo <u>four</u> the animals.

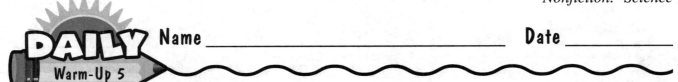

Name _____ **Date** _____

AMPHIBIANS

Do you think that only fish can live in the water? It is not true. Other kinds of animals can live there, too. They are called amphibians.

These are animals that can live in the water, and they can also live on land.

Most of them hatch out of eggs. Frogs and toads hatch from eggs. They live in the water and on land.

They also have smooth, wet skin. This means that they have to live close to water so they will not get too dry. If their skin gets too dry, they will die. They will not be able to live.

All of them have legs. When they are on land, they move around by hopping or walking.

Can you think of one that hops, has wet skin, and lives on land and in the water?

STORY QUESTIONS

1. How are amphibians not like fish?
a. They can only live in the water.
b. They can all go to school.
c. They can live in the water and on land.
d. They can only live on land.

2. How do they move when they are on land?
a. biking or jumping
b. swimming or jumping
c. hopping or walking
d. skipping or jumping

3. If an amphibian's skin was too dry, what would happen?
a. It would jump in a lake.
b. Nothing would happen.
c. It would be sad.
d. It would die.

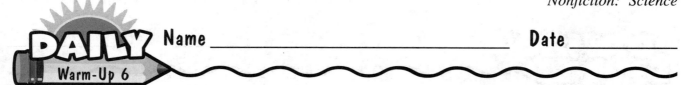

INSECTS

Did you know that insects are animals that do not have bones inside?

Insects are small. They are not like fish, and they are not like reptiles. They are not like birds. Their babies do not look like them at all. Most of the babies look like worms.

All insects have six legs. Most insects can fly. They have wings.

Some of them have a hard shell on the outside of their body. This shell helps to keep them safe.

Most people think some insects are cute. Ladybugs and butterflies are ones that people like. Bees and beetles are insects that many people think are not very pretty.

Insects are in the world we live in. They are in the garden. They are in the desert. They are in the hills. There is no place where you will go and not see at least one insect.

STORY QUESTIONS

1. Which of these sentences is **NOT** a fact about insects?
   a. Some live in gardens.
   b. Most of them can fly.
   c. They live in water.
   d. They have wings.

2. How are insects different from other animals?
   a. Kids love them.
   b. They live in schools.
   c. They have no bones.
   d. They can play baseball.

3. How many legs do insects have?
   a. seven
   b. six
   c. four
   d. eight

DAILY Name _____ Date _____

Warm-Up 7

SEEDS

Did you know that all plants start with a seed? They do. Some seeds are big. Some seeds are small, but they are all the start of a plant. Seeds can come in many colors.

Watermelons have many seeds. The seeds are flat and black. They look like teardrops. These seeds feel slimy and wet.

Peach seeds are not <u>small</u>. They are big and oval. They have many holes. They feel rough to your fingers. Peach seeds look like Mars.

Apples have seeds that are small. They are brown. Apple seeds are long and shaped like a teardrop. They are a little puffy and are not flat.

Plants all have seeds, but all of the seeds look different from each other. They make plants that are different. They make our world a pretty place.

STORY QUESTIONS

1. Antonyms are words that mean the opposite. What is an antonym for the word *small?*

a. rich

b. quickly

c. tiny

d. large

2. What is the job of a seed?

a. to make friends in the park

b. to start a new plant

c. to sit on a desk

d. to bug other seeds

3. How are apple seeds and watermelon seeds like each other?

a. They are the same size.

b. They are the same shape.

c. They both can make apples grow.

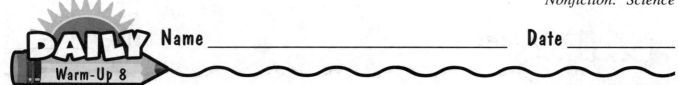

Name _____ Date _____

HABITATS

What do you call the place where plants and animals live? It is called a "habitat." There are many kinds of habitats.

Animals need to eat the plants for food. Plants need the animals to make more plants. They have to live in one place and help each other.

Some live in the desert. Deserts are dry and hot. There is only a little water. It is hot in the day and cool at night. Not much moves in the day. It is too hot.

Forests are wet and damp. The leaves are big and green. Animals can drink a lot of water. Trees can get water for their roots. It is a busy place in the daytime.

Lakes are another place for animals to live. The lakes have water. Mud and weeds are in the lake. Ducks swim in the mud. Worms dig in and out of the mud. Weeds grow tall. They blow in the wind.

The world has many places for animals to live. The desert, the forest, and the lake are only a few of the places they can live.

STORY QUESTIONS

1. Why do animals in a habitat need the plants?
   a. for houses
   b. for food
   c. for playing games
   d. for building nests

2. Which of these is not a habitat?
   a. ice cream
   b. desert
   c. ocean
   d. forest

3. If you visited the desert in the day, what do you think you should wear?
   a. mittens and a hat
   c. shorts and a tank top
   b. boots and a coat
   d. swimsuit and goggles

DAILY Warm-Up 9

Name _____ Date _____

SEASONS

The sun gives light to the earth. It makes our weather change from day to day. Some of the time, it is sunny. Other days are cloudy. Some days are rainy. Other days are snowy or windy. It is always changing. The weather changes during the seasons.

In summer the sun is closest to the earth. It is warm and sunny. People like to swim and go to the beach. They like to play in the sand and eat drink cold soda. They like to put their toes in the sand.

Fall is when the leaves fall off the trees. They turn colors: red, green, orange, and brown. Things start to die and turn brown. The wind starts to blow. It starts to get colder every day, and people wear coats.

Winter is the coldest time of all. The leaves have fallen off the trees. Some places have snow. Other places just feel colder than in the fall. Plants do not grow. Trees sit empty. The nests have no eggs. Birds fly away.

Spring comes. The flowers come back. Leaves grow on the trees. Things start to get green again. The sun shines behind the clouds. Summer is near.

STORY QUESTIONS

1. What is one thing we know that is **TRUE** about the weather?
   a. It is always changing.
   b. It is always sunny.
   c. It is always rainy.
   d. It is always hot.

2. Why should we look outside before we get dressed?
   a. So we can write stories.
   b. So we can take pictures.
   c. So we can find out what we should put on.
   d. So we can read books.

3. What will you most likely see in the winter?
   a. people having picnics in the snow   c. an empty bird nest
   b. green leaves   d. people playing in the water

EARTH'S RESOURCES

The earth gives us things we need. These things are called <u>resources</u>. People use these things every day. We have three resources that the earth gives us: water, land, and air.

People need clean water to drink. We need it to brush our teeth. We need it to take a bath. Clean water is good for washing our clothes. It is good for washing our cars. It is good for playing in. Clean water makes us feel fresh and clean.

We need air, too. We need clean air to breathe. We need it to make our bodies stay healthy. We need it to grow plants. We need clean air so animals will stay alive.

We also need land. It is a good place to grow food. It is a good place to build homes. It is used to make landfills. This is a place where people take their trash, so that it does not make us sick. It is good to take care of our land. We need to keep it clean.

Land, water, and air are all things we must have to be safe and grow strong.

STORY QUESTIONS

1. What are *resources*?
   a. brushes to clean our teeth
   b. a group of animals
   c. things from the earth that we need

2. What are the three resources the earth gives us?
   a. stars, ice cream, and cookies
   b. land, oranges, and apples
   c. water, land, air
   d. air, snow, and water

3. We need water for . . .
   a. keeping clean and brushing our teeth.
   b. breathing.
   c. building houses.
   d. picking up trash.

DAILY Name _____   Date _____
Warm-Up 1

WINTER OLYMPICS

In 2006, the Winter Olympics were held in Italy. People from all over the world came to try to win the games. They came in cars. They came on trains. Some came in buses. Others came in planes.

Some of them came to ski. Others came to skate. Some came to play hockey. Others came to snowboard.

They came <u>hoping</u> to win gold medals. They wanted to take them back to their homes. They were hoping to show their parents and friends how good they were. Each of them came hoping that they would be the best.

Most of the people worked for four years to go to the Olympics. Each of them trained to be the best they could be. Some got medals. Others did not. They worked hard, and they raced hard. They also played hard.

The best of the best got to take home the gold.

STORY QUESTIONS

1. Why did people want to go to the Olympics?
   a. to find new friends
   b. to win medals
   c. to see new places
   d. to try new foods

2. A **synonym** is a word that means the same thing. *Hoping* means to . . .
   a. give up.
   b. not care at all.
   c. want something very badly.
   d. not try hard.

3. What guess can we make about the people who came to the Olympics?
   a. Some will go home with medals. Others will go home with no medals.
   b. They will all get medals.
   c. They will all be happy.

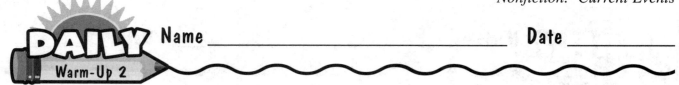

Name _____ Date _____

IPOD

Do you like music? Do you want to hear songs? There is a new music box. It is called the iPod®.

It is very small. The iPod is as small as a candy bar. It is as thin as a CD case. It has a small window on the front that shows you the song that is playing. You can push the arrows up or down to move to your choice of songs. You can pick the song you want to hear.

The iPod can hold more songs than any other music player. It can hold at least 5,000 songs. It keeps the songs inside. You can listen for a long time. <u>You could hear music all day.</u> It will just keep playing and playing. It can play music for at least 15 hours and will not need to stop.

The iPod costs money. One is over $250 dollars.

The iPods are always changing. The newer iPods can hold pictures and videos. It is also very strong. If you drop it, it will still be okay.

The iPod is a great new music player for anyone. Who knows what the next iPods will look like?

STORY QUESTIONS

1. Which is **NOT TRUE** about the iPod?
   a. It costs at least $250.00
   b. It is very small.
   c. It holds only 200 songs.
   d. It plays music for a very long time.

2. The words "You could hear music all day" mean that . . .
   a. it plays in a circle.
   b. it plays songs that are old.
   c. you can not turn it off.
   d. the music goes on and on.

3. The iPod is as small as a _____.
   a. a candy bar
   b. CD case
   c. a stamp

DAILY
Warm-Up 3

Name _____   Date _____

HURRICANE KATRINA

Hurricane Katrina started on August 23, 2005. It was a big storm. It had strong winds. It was one of the biggest storms in history.

Many people were told to pack their bags. They were told to get into their cars. They were told to go to other cities.

Some people did what they were told. They drove away and were <u>safe</u>.

Many people did not want to go. They said they would not go away from their homes. They thought they would be safe.

The storm came, and it was very bad. It was worse than they thought. They were not safe. There was water all over the city. The wind blew houses away. It blew cars down the street. Many stores were gone.

Hurricane Katrina did not care about the people. She was a strong storm. She blew and blew. She made a big mess and then she left a mess for the people to clean up.

STORY QUESTIONS

1. An **antonym** is a word that means the opposite. What is an antonym for *safe*?
   a. unsafe
   b. bad
   c. ugly
   d. mean

2. Why did some of the people die in the storm?
   a. They got stuck under cars.
   b. They went to wrong hotel.
   c. They did not leave when they were told.
   d. They had too many things with them.

3. Which word best describes Hurricane Katrina?
   a. strong
   b. nice
   c. soft

DAILY Name _____ Date _____
Warm-Up 4

TSUNAMI

In December of 2005, there were big waves in the ocean. They were too big. They hit many places on the land. These waves were called tsunami waves.

It was Christmas morning. Visitors were in their hotels. Many people had opened their gifts.

A big wave came to the shore. It was the biggest one that had been seen. Some people got their cameras. Others got scared and started to run.

No one knew that is was going to be so big. No one knew that it would make the hotels fall down.

The waves hit hard. They tossed people like sticks of wood. Beach chairs went flying into the air. The water was moving very fast. It was full of things.

The waves <u>stopped</u>. People looked for the people they loved. Some of them were alive. Others were missing. Some were dead. It was a very sad day.

The big waves had washed over the islands. They had washed over cities. They were <u>gone</u> and would never come back.

STORY QUESTIONS

1. What is a tsunami?
   a. strong winds
   b. small waves
   c. big waves that start under the ocean
   d. large boats

2. A **synonym** is a word that means the same thing. Which word is a synonym for the word *gone*?
   a. washed   c. over
   b. hiding   d. missing

3. The word *stopped* is . . .
   a. future tense.
   b. present tense.
   c. past tense.

Name _____ Date _____

TOUR DE FRANCE

Lance Armstrong is a brave man. In 2005, he rode in the bike race. It is called Tour de France. He won the race.

Lance wanted to win this race badly. He wanted to win, because it was his last time to ride in this race.

He is a very good bike rider. Lance is the best bike rider in the world. He won the Tour de France seven times. He won for seven years in a row. No one has ever done that before.

Lance was also happy because he has also won another race. It was the race with cancer. A few years ago, he got very sick. He did not want to die. He did what the doctor said to do. He kept riding his bike. He kept fighting cancer.

Lance says to "Fight or quit." He did not quit. He decided to fight. He won. Now, he is the winner of both things: cancer and the bike race.

STORY QUESTIONS

1. What word talks about Lance Armstrong?
  a. weak
  b. scared
  c. mean
  d. brave

2. If Lance talked to you, he would say, . . .
  a. "It's not the end of the world."
  b. "Today is another day."
  c. "Never stop trying!"
  d. "Don't worry. Be happy!"

3. How many times did Lance win the Tour de France?
  a. six   c. three
  b. seven   d. five

Name _____   Date _____

SEPTEMBER 11TH

Do your parents ever talk to you about 9/11? That is a date in history. On September 11, 2001, two planes hit the World Trade Center towers. These towers were in New York City. Another plane crashed in Washington, D.C. A third plane crashed in Pennsylvania. Many people died that day. These crashes were not accidents. They were done on purpose. People who did not like the United States caused the crashes.

Even now, people still feel sad about what happened that day. Each year, on September 11th, people do different things to show how they remember. One boy makes red, white, and blue key chains. He sells them to raise money for firefighters from 9/11. A girl writes to the police and firefighters. She thanks them for saving lives. Another boy says he hugs his mom and dad extra hard and says, "I love you." One woman decided to make quilts dedicated to each person who died.

September 11th was a very sad day. Many lives were lost. People who remember the victims want to keep their memories strong. There is a saying you might hear sometimes when people talk about 9/11. They say, "We will never forget."

STORY QUESTIONS

1. In this story, what is 9/11?
   a. a fraction
   b. the final score of a soccer game
   c. the height of a basketball player
   d. a date in history

2. Where did two of the planes crash on 9/11?
   a. San Francisco
   b. New York City
   c. Los Angeles
   d. Florida

3. What do you think would be a word people use to describe September 11th?
   a. peaceful
   b. happy
   c. sad
   d. excited

DAILY Name _____ Date _____
Warm-Up 7

JOHN PAUL II DIES

John Paul II was the pope for the Catholic Church. A pope is a man who is the big boss of the church. He tells people to do things that are right. He tells people to love God.

John Paul worked for a very long time. He was the pope for 27 years. John Paul did a lot of work for the church. He had to work many long hours.

John Paul wanted people to work as a team. He wanted them to care about each other. He wanted them to be kind. He told people to help others who did not have as much as they did.

He got sick in 1992, but he did not stop working. He kept doing his job. He kept talking to people about God. He kept telling them to be kind to others. John Paul did not get better. On April 2, 2005, he died.

Many people were sad. Many people loved him. They went to Rome to say good-bye. They wanted to tell him they would do their best to be kind to others.

STORY QUESTIONS

1. What pope has had the job for 27 years?
   a. Frank Glenn II
   b. John Paul III
   c. John Paul II
   d. George Bush III

2. When he got sick, what did John Paul do?
   a. He kept working.
   b. He took a vacation.
   c. He gave up his job.
   d. He quit trying to help the world.

3. What did John Paul care about?
   a. going to the park   c. being sick
   b. having a good time   d. being kind to others

DAILY
Warm-Up 8

Name _____ Date _____

BEN

Ben Roethlisberger is a football star. He plays for a team called the Steelers. Ben is 23 years old. He is big, and he is tall. Ben is very strong and very fast.

Ben has played for two years. Ben threw the ball 268 times in a year. Other players caught 168 of the balls that he threw. He made 17 touchdowns. Every time he ran, he ran about eight yards. He played 13 games in a year.

Mothers and fathers like to watch Ben play. Kids like to watch Ben play. People just want to see Ben. If he is hurt, they still want to see him sitting on the bench. If he is playing, they want to yell his name.

They want to buy shirts with his name on them. They want to go to his games. People are talking about "Ben" all over the U.S.

Ben is a great player. He has many years left to play. He will be even better next year! We know that for sure!

STORY QUESTIONS

1. What makes Ben great?
   a. He is a great player, and he is very young.
   b. He is ugly.
   c. He has blond hair.
   d. He can play soccer.

2. How many times did he pass the ball in a year?
   a. 178
   b. 168
   c. 13
   d. 268

3. On which team did Ben play?
   a. Steelers
   b. Panthers
   c. Knicks

AIR FORCE ONE

Did you know you could see an important plane? It is a plane for seven presidents. These men used this plane to take them to many places. They sat in the chairs. They slept in the beds. They ate in this plane. Some of them even played golf in this plane.

This plane is at the Ronald Reagan Museum. It is in Simi Valley, California. It came there in October 2005.

A room was made for the plane. It has glass windows on all of the sides. The plane is in the middle of the room.

People can come and see the plane. They can walk up the stairs. They can stand and wave. They can act like they are in the president's family. A man or a lady will take their photos.

They can walk inside. They can see where the presidents worked. They can see where they slept. They can see where they ate.

<u>It is fun to walk on the plane.</u> It makes you feel good to walk where presidents have walked.

STORY QUESTIONS

1. Why did people come to see the plane?
   a. It was old.
   b. It was big.
   c. They came to eat at the snack bar.
   d. It had taken seven presidents on trips around the world.

2. What can people who go to the museum do?
   a. ride in the plane
   b. walk in the plane
   c. cook in the plane
   d. take a nap in the plane

3. Tell what kind of sentence this is: <u>It is fun to walk on the plane.</u>
   a. exclamatory
   b. interrogative
   c. declarative

Name _____ Date _____

LION KING TRYOUTS

This year there is going to be a show. It is going to be like the movie *The Lion King*. The show will move from place to place.

The people who are doing the show are looking for kids to be stars. The kids have to be able to sing. They cannot be too tall. If they were taller than 58 inches, they were too tall. They cannot be short either. They cannot be too young. All of the kids have to be 9, 10, 11, or 12 years old.

About 700 kids came to try out for the parts. They learned to dance. They learned to act. They sang the songs. They had to learn all the words to the song. The kids are trying out to play Nala or Simba. They are trying to sing in the choir.

The kids who get picked will make $1,381 dollars a week. They will travel and be very busy. It will be hard work, but they will have fun.

STORY QUESTIONS

1. What **compound word** means "to try to do something"?
   a. underdog
   b. something
   c. tryouts
   d. inside

2. What movie will the play be like?
   a. *The King and I*
   b. *Nala and Simba*
   c. *Sing and Dance*
   d. *The Lion King*

3. How many kids tried to get a part in the show?
   a. about 700   c. about 600
   b. about 200   d. about 1,000

Name _____ Date _____

FIVE MUMMIES

In January of 2006, archaeologists found a new tomb. Archaeologists are people who find old things. They study them. They give us clues to the past.

The tomb was in Egypt. There were five mummies inside. Lots of other things were there, too. Mud huts were not far away from the tomb. These huts were for the workers who built the tomb. There were long dirt holes dug in the ground. They went all the way inside.

The mummies had brown cloth over them. The cloth was on top of the bodies. They were very old. Each mummy had a mask on its face. One of them was not good. It was falling into little pieces.

This tomb is in the Valley of the Kings. It is not a tomb for a king, but they think it is for a friend of the king. The king must have liked him very much to let them be buried in the Valley of the Kings.

There are pictures on the wall. The pictures will give us clues about the people who are in the tomb and tell us about their life.

The archaelogists must dig fast. Soon it will be too hot to work. It will be too hot to find more things. They must move the things out of the tomb by May. After that, they can look at the cloths and the mummies. They can study them in a place that is not too hot to work.

STORY QUESTIONS

1. What is the name for a person who studies things from the past?
   a. doctor
   b. lawyer
   c. teacher
   d. archaeologist

2. Why did they have to dig fast?
   a. It is not a good place to dig.   c. It is getting too cold.
   b. It is getting too hot.   d. It has too much sand.

3. Why do archaeologists study things from long ago?
   a. so they can write books for money
   b. so they can tell stories about the things they find
   c. so they can be happy
   d. so they can find out what life was like long ago

DAILY Warm-Up 12   Name _____   Date _____

WORKING IN THE MINES

All over the world, there are men in mines. They are called miners. They work under the ground. They put coal into cars. Others dig for iron. Each miner digs and digs. Miners move the coal or iron. They move the gold or silver.

When it is ready, they take it out of the ground. The gold or silver is sent away to be sold. The iron is sent away, and the coal is sent away, too.

In 2005 and 2006, there have been many bad days in the mines. Men have been doing their jobs, but the walls have fallen in. Men have gotten stuck under the ground.

Some of them had air to breathe. Others ran out of air in the holes. Others ran to get out, but some could not get out. Rocks would fall, and wood crashed. Things did not go well.

Working in a mine is a hard job. It is not very safe. These men are brave. They go down in the ground day after day.

Being a miner is hard. They make a lot of money, but they have to be brave to do the job.

STORY QUESTIONS

1. What guess can you make about working in a mine?
   a. They have lots of light under the ground.
   b. It is not scary at all.
   c. It is easy.
   d. It is not the safest job.

2. How are miners and groundhogs the same?
   a. They both ride up and down in cars.
   b. They both like to eat lunch at 12:00.
   c. They spend a lot of time in tunnels under the ground.
   d. They both make a lot of money.

3. If you are scared of small, dark places, you do not want to be a . . .
   a. teacher.   c. cop.
   b. truck driver.   d. miner.

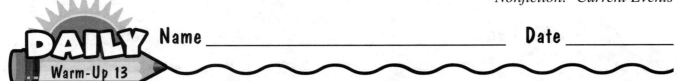

Name _____   Date _____

MOMS AND DADS WANT KIDS TO EAT VEGGIES

In Texas, moms and dads are trying something new. They are doing a test at school.

Kids are not eating good food. Many of them are getting fat. They are eating things that are not good for them, and they are not eating their veggies.

Moms and Dad are not happy. The schools are not happy. They had an idea. They can pay for the lunches before the kids eat them. They can say if they want them to eat junk food. They can say if there are things they cannot eat. They can say if there are foods that make the child sick.

The child <u>goes</u> to school. When he or she goes to lunch, he or she punches a number. The machine looks at the food. If the child has things that mom and dad say he or she cannot eat, the lady puts the food back.

Some people like the idea. They think it is good. Other people do not like it. They do not worry about the things their children eat.

It is only a test, but it is working for some schools. It is making the children be more careful when they eat.

STORY QUESTIONS

1. What are some parents worried about?
   a. that kids do not like recess
   b. that kids are getting bad grades
   c. that kids are eating too many things that are bad for them

2. An **antonym** is a word that means the opposite. An antonym for the word *goes* would be . . .
   a. leave.
   b. went.
   c. stays.
   d. left.

3. How do the people feel about the test?
   a. They all like it.
   b. Some like it. Others don't.
   c. No one likes it at all.

DAILY
Warm-Up 14

Name _____ Date _____

SPACE SHUTTLE COMES HOME

August 10, 2005, was a good day for space. It was a good day for NASA. NASA is the agency that makes rockets. It is the place that studies space.

It was a good day for the astronauts on the space shuttle. They were coming home.

For over two years, no space shuttles had gone to space. The last one had come apart in the sky. All of the people on it had died.

Today the *Discovery* was coming back to Earth. It was raining in many places. It was stormy. It was not safe to land.

NASA said to try to land at Edwards Air Force Base. It was in the desert. It was far away from Florida. There were only small bushes and dirt.

It was the best place to land. Things were just right. The astronauts looked out the window. The earth got closer and closer. The wheels came down. They were ready to come home.

Touchdown. They landed on the ground. They were safe. The shuttle was safe. They were home.

STORY QUESTIONS

1. What is NASA?
   a. an agency that makes rockets
   b. a factory that makes toys
   c. a beach

2. Why did the shuttle have to go to Edwards Air Force Base in California?
   a. It was the safest place to land.
   b. It had the best runway.
   c. It was close to Florida.
   d. It was stormy there.

3. A different title for this passage would be . . .
   a. "The Rocket Is Not Coming"
   b. "A Day to be Happy!"
   c. "People Are Sad"
   d. "The Desert"

FICTION

Contemporary Realistic Fiction

Mystery/Suspense/Adventure

Historical Fiction

Fantasy

Fairy Tales/Folklore

88

DAILY Warm-Up 1   Name _____   Date _____

BARNELLA

Once upon a time, there was a farmer.

"My name is Fred. I have a wife, and I have a daughter. My daughter's name is Polly."

"We have a farm, and we have two tractors. It is a happy life," said the wife.

One sad day, Polly's mother died.

"I will get a new wife," said her father.

The new wife was mean. She did not like Polly.

One day her dad went to town in his blue truck. "I will be home in time for dinner," he said. He kissed Polly.

They called Polly, "Barnella." They made her do many chores.

Pokey was the oldest stepsister. She said, "Barnella, clean the barn."

Picky was the youngest. She said, "Barnella, get the eggs."

The stepmother said, "Barnella, get my socks. Barnella, sweep the dirt."

Polly was sad. She cried. Polly went to the barn.

Her father came home. He looked for Polly. She was under the haystack.

"They are mean," she said.

"Let's go," said her father.

They went into the house. Polly packed a bag, and Dad packed a bag. They left for a short trip in the blue truck. Polly felt better after spending time with her dad.

STORY QUESTIONS

1. Where did Polly's dad go?
    a. He went to the park.   c. He went to the bank.
    b. He went to town.   d. He went to the store.

2. Why was Polly so upset?
    a. Her stepsisters were treating her badly.
    b. She missed her dad.
    c. She couldn't ride in the blue truck.
    d. She wanted chicken for dinner.

3. What fairy tale is this like?
    a. "Three Little Pigs"   c. "Jack and the Beanstalk"
    b. "Cinderella"

Name _____   Date _____

THREE LITTLE BUGS

It was a sunny day. Three little bugs packed a bag.

"Goodbye, Mother," said Joe. "I will go to the city."

"Goodbye, Joe. Be a good boy," said his mother.

"Goodbye, Mom," said Seth. "I will go to the hills."

"Goodbye, Seth," said Mother. "Please, be good."

"Goodbye, Mother," said Sage. "I will go to the country."

"Goodbye, Sage. Be good," said Mother.

They all kissed her goodbye.

Joe had a blue bag and a hat.

Seth had a green bag and two toys.

Sage had a red bag. Sage took books. He took a saw to cut wood.

Joe went to the city. Seth went to the hills. Sage went to the country.

Joe made a house of sticks. It was small. The door was not big.

Seth made a house of weeds. It had no windows. It had one door.

Sage made a house of bricks. He made a roof out of wood. Sage made a wall.

One day the wolf came to find bugs for his lunch. He blew Joe's house down. He blew Seth's house down. He could not blow Sage's house down. He gave up blowing and went home to eat soup.

STORY QUESTIONS

1. Which words tell us about Sage?

a. He is mean.

b. He is quick.

c. He is sloppy.

d. He is careful and plans ahead.

2. How was Sage different than his brothers?

a. He was smarter.

b. He was lazy.

c. He was not sleepy.

d. He liked to draw.

3. What fairy tale is this like?

a. "Goldilocks and the Three Bears"

b. "Three Little Pigs"

c. "Cinderella"

d. "Jack and the Beanstalk"

DAILY Warm-Up 3   Name _____   Date _____

SAVANNAH AND THE GIANT SUNFLOWER

Savannah lived in a little town. She had a mother and a father. She had one brother. One rainy day her mother gave her $3.00.

"Buy milk at the store," said mother.

"I will," said Savannah. "I will get the milk for you."

She put on her purple rain boots. Savannah put on her purple rain coat. She put on her purple rain hat. Then she left for the store.

Her friend was walking, too. He had on blue boots. He had on a blue hat, and his rain coat was blue.

"Hello, Savannah. Where are you going?"

"I am going to the store. I will buy milk for my mother. I have three dollars."

"I have a magic sunflower plant."

"How much is it?"

"It is three dollars."

Savannah gave him the three dollars. She took the plant and went home. Her mom was mad. She threw it out the window.

From that plant a tall sunflower plant grew. It went to the sky.

STORY QUESTIONS

1. Which color does Savannah like best?
   a. blue
   b. purple
   c. brown
   d. red

2. Which **compound word** from the story means "a big flower that likes the sun"?
   a. sunflower
   b. raindrop
   c. butterfly
   d. racecar

3. What fairy tale is this like?
   a. "Three Little Pigs"
   b. "Jack and the Beanstalk'
   c. "Sleeping Beauty"

DAILY Warm-Up 4

Name _____ Date _____

TINY, BLACK COW

Parker was a tiny, black cow. He lived on a big farm.

Katie was his friend. She lived on the farm.

Spencer lived on the farm, too.

Parker did all the work. He got the eggs. At night, he fed the dogs. He made the food. All he did was work.

"I want cookies," said Katie. She sat in her chair.

"I want cake," said Spencer.

Parker worked and worked. He was getting tired of working. His friends were lazy. He made a plan.

One stormy day, he made a big cake. It was chocolate. It had frosting. The cake looked great!

All his friends wanted to eat it.

"Not this time," said Parker. "I will eat it myself."

He ate it all by himself. The friends could not have one bite. They were mad.

"You have to help out!" said Parker. "You have to work, too."

Now, they all do chores. And, they all eat cake!

STORY QUESTIONS

1. What was Parker always doing?
   a. playing in the yard
   b. sitting in the chair
   c. laying in the grass
   d. working on the farm

2. What was Parker trying to teach his friends?
   a. to help with the chores
   b. how to make a cake
   c. how to milk cows
   d. how to feed the dogs

3. What fairy tale is this like?
   a. "Three Little Pigs"
   b. "Little Red Hen"
   c. "Little Red Riding Hood"

DAILY
Warm-Up 5

Name _____

Date _____

THE HORSES AND THE TROLL

Kerry was the oldest horse in the family. He was six years old. He liked to work with his hands. Kerry was small, but he was smart.

Tim was the second oldest brother. He was four. Tim loved to read books. He was strong and tough.

Nate was the baby brother. He was very smart. Nate liked to play games.

Every day the three brothers loved to eat grass.

One day they met a mean troll who owned the bridge. He made them pay $1.00 a day to cross the bridge so they could eat grass on the other side.

One morning the grass was not good. It tasted sour. It tasted dry. The brothers were mad. They wanted to go home early, but the troll stopped them. He wanted to eat them for lunch.

He tried to eat Kerry, but he made a boat and crossed to the other side.

He wanted to eat Tim, but he was too tough to chew. His tail was like rubber.

When Nate came along, the troll tried to eat him, but Nate said they must play a game first. If the troll won, he could eat Nate for lunch. If Nate won, then he would not have to pay $1.00 each day.

Nate won the game. The three brothers never had to pay $1.00 again. The troll was mad and had to buy a new bridge.

STORY QUESTIONS

1. Which best describes the troll?
   a. mean
   b. kind
   c. caring
   d. quiet

2. Which of the three brothers liked to play games?
   a. Tim
   b. Kerry
   c. Nate
   d. Troll

3. What fairy tale is this like?
   a. "Three Little Pigs"
   b. "Three Billy Goats Gruff"
   c. "Goldilocks and the Three Bears"

DAILY Warm-Up 6 Name _____ Date _____

ESSIE AND THE PARROTS

It was a hot day. The sun was shining on the trees. All the leaves were bright green. Mother Parrot, Father Parrot, and Baby Parrot wanted to take a walk. They packed a lunch and went to the park.

Essie was a little girl. She had red hair, and her legs were short. She liked to find new things. That morning, she was taking a walk.

"What is this I see?" she said. "It looks like a <u>pretty</u> little house. It is painted green. It has vines on the windows. It has a blue door. I think I will go in."

Essie knocked on the door. She pushed it open and went in. The house was empty. It had three green chairs. There were three stools in the kitchen. Three beds were upstairs. Three glasses of juice were in the kitchen.

The tallest glass was too big. The medium-sized glass was too sweet. The baby glass tasted just right. She drank it all up.

Essie was tired. She walked upstairs. The big bed was too lumpy. The medium bed was too soft. The baby bed was just right. Essie pulled up the covers and went right to sleep.

STORY QUESTIONS

1. An **antonym** is a word that means the opposite. An antonym for *pretty* would be . . .
   a. handsome.
   b. good looking.
   c. beautiful.
   d. ugly.

2. Why did Essie drink the little juice?
   a. It tasted just right.   c. It was too sweet.
   b. It was too sour.   d. It was too big.

3. What fairy tale is this like?
   a. "Cinderella"
   b. "Goldilocks and the Three Bears"
   c. "Three Little Pigs"

Name _____ Date _____

LARS AND NINA

Lars and Nina lived in France. Their father and mother lived in a small cottage. Lars loved to hunt in the woods with his father. Nina liked to cook bread with her mother in the kitchen. They were happy.

One day Nina's and Lars' mother got very sick. She died, and Lars' father married another wife. She did not like Lars and Nina at all. The new wife was mean to them. She made them eat hard rolls. She made them sleep in the barn.

One day she told the father to take them out to the woods.

"Do not bring them back. I want the house for just the two of us!"

The father was sad. He took them to the woods. Lars and Nina did not know their father would leave them in the woods. Their father said he would not be back, and they cried.

Nina and Lars then went to look for another place to live. They found a small house in the woods. It had candy on the windows. Gum was on the doors. The walls were made of chocolate. It looked very good.

They knocked at the door. A kind lady answered the door. She fed them supper. Her name was Tanja. Her husband had died. They stayed with Tanja. She sent them to school. She taught them to read and write. Nina, Lars, and Tanja were happy forever.

STORY QUESTIONS

1. Why were the children left in the woods?
   a. The new stepmother didn't want them.
   b. They got lost.
   c. They were camping.
   d. They were playing hide and seek.

2. Out of what is the house in the woods made?
   a. It is made out of veggies.   c. It is made out of mints.
   b. It is made out of ice cream.   d. It is made out of candy.

3. What fairy tale is this like?
   a. "Cinderella"
   b. "Hansel and Gretel"
   c. "Snow White"

DAILY
Warm-Up 8

Name _____

Date _____

RAIN BLUE

"Mirror, Mirror, on the wall, who is the prettiest one of all?" asked the queen.

"Rain Blue," answered the mirror.

The queen was angry. She hit the mirror, and she screamed. It was not a good day for the queen.

"Where is Rain Blue?" she asked the mirror.

"She is in the cottage of the seven little bees. They live in the middle of the forest."

The queen put on a wig. She put on a funny dress and very big shoes. She put a wart on her nose. Over her head she wore a big, blue hat with feathers. In a basket were poisonous bananas.

"I will find Rain Blue!" she yelled.

The seven little bees went to work in the morning.

"Lock the door, Rain Blue. Do not talk to strangers," they said.

"I won't. Thank you." Rain Blue shut the door. She dusted the house, and then she read a book.

Rain Blue started to sing when she heard a knock at the door. It was the queen dressed up. She asked Rain Blue if she would like a banana.

Rain Blue said, "No, thank you. I just ate my lunch, and I am not hungry anymore."

The queen went away angry.

STORY QUESTIONS

1. What did the queen want to know?
   a. who was the ugliest
   b. who was the fattest
   c. who was the meanest
   d. who was the prettiest

2. The seven little bees did not want Rain Blue to be hurt. They said, . . .
   a. "Do not talk to strangers."
   b. "Do not eat bananas."
   c. "Always look at the sky."
   d. "Stay out of trouble."

3. What fairy tale is this like?
   a. "Cinderella"
   b. "Three Little Pigs"
   c. "Snow White"

DAILY Warm-Up 9   Name _____ Date _____

THE RAT AND THE PRINCESS

Mia was a princess. She lived in a big, blue castle. Her dad painted purple and yellow flowers on the walls. The halls had green leaves and green carpet. She was spoiled.

"I want to wear my pink dress! I want my purple shoes! Give me my tea set! Where are my dolls?" she yelled.

One day she took her dolls to the garden. They had tea. She dropped her teapot in a hole.

"Who will get my teapot?" she asked.

"I will," said the little rat.

"You are too ugly," she said.

"I will get it anyway," said the rat. "You must take me home with you."

He got the teapot, and the princess went home. She left the rat in the garden.

He followed her home. She did not like him, so she <u>threw</u> him into the pond. Suddenly, he became a prince! The princess saw he was a nice prince so she married him. They lived happily ever after.

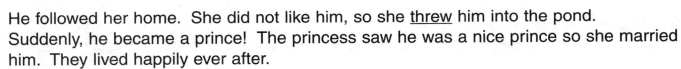

STORY QUESTIONS

1. A **synonym** is a word that means the same. A synonym for the word *threw* is . . .
   a. caught.   c. tossed.
   b. grabbed.   d. held.

2. Why was the princess outside?
   a. She was having a tea party.
   b. She was having a swimming party.
   c. She wanted to catch rats.
   d. She wanted to pick flower in her garden.

3. What fairy tale is this like?
   a. "Three Billy Goats Gruff"   c. "Three Little Pigs"
   b. "Hansel and Gretel"   d. "The Princess and the Frog"

DAILY
Warm-Up 10

Name _____   Date _____

SLOW WORM AND THE QUAIL

Brianna was a worm. She was very slow but always finished what she started. Brianna loved to be with her friends. She loved to read, and she loved to write and do math.

Allyssa lived in the next house. She was a quail. Allyssa ran very fast. She was in a hurry all the time and made many mistakes. Her life was busy, busy, busy.

On Monday, they went to the park for a picnic.

"Let's have race," said Allyssa.

"I think that would be a great idea," said Brianna. "I am sure I can beat you."

"No way!" yelled Allyssa. "I am very fast!"

"We will see," said Brianna. "We will see."

On Tuesday, the animals came to the park. Allyssa had on a new gym suit. Brianna had on new running shorts. They were ready for the race.

"Good luck," said the judge.

"Good luck," said their friends.

STORY QUESTIONS

1. What was Allyssa wearing in the race?
   a. an old shirt
   b. a new gym suit
   c. new shorts
   d. a dress

2. Why do you think Brianna will win the race?
   a. She always finishes what she starts.
   b. She won't.
   c. She loves to read.
   d. She has a new gym suit.

3. What fairy tale is this like?
   a. "The Tortoise and the Hare"
   b. "Jack and the Beanstalk"
   c. "Snow White"

Name _____ Date _____

UGLY MONKEY

Mother monkey was very surprised when she came back to the cave. She had three babies and not two. One of the babies was white. It did not have a monkey nose. It did not have a monkey tail. The eyes did not look like monkey eyes. It did not sound like a monkey.

She did not think it was a monkey, but she kept it anyway.

Every day she fed him. She fed him what monkeys eat. Momma played monkey games with him, too. She talked to him in monkey words.

When Momma was not looking, the two monkeys made fun of the white baby.

"You are ugly," they said. "You are white, and you talk funny."

The white baby was sad. He cried, but he still tried to be nice. Momma monkey loved him anyway.

One day the zookeeper came in the cage. She saw three babies. She then called her boss. <u>He came running!</u> They called 911.

It was not a baby monkey in the cage. It was a pretty baby boy.

STORY QUESTIONS

1. Tell what kind of sentence this is: <u>He came running!</u>
   a. none of these
   b. declarative
   c. interrogative
   d. exclamatory

2. How was white baby different from the other monkey babies?
   a. He had fur.
   b. He had hair all over his body.
   c. He talked in monkey talk.
   d. He was a human baby.

3. What fairy tale is this like?
   a. "The Ugly Duckling"
   b. "Hansel and Gretel"
   c. "Snow White"
   d. "The Princess and the Frog"

Name _____   Date _____

THE APPLE GIRL

A city had a king. He was very mean, and the people did not like him. He made all the people give him their best apples.

One day the king rode around the city. He took all the best apples from the people. He even took the apples from the poor.

One poor man had a daughter. He wanted her to have a good life. He wanted his daughter to live in the great palace. He then thought of an idea.

When the king's wagon had stopped, he told his daughter to jump into the wagon and hide under a basket of apples. He kissed her goodbye and wished her well. He then covered her with apples so no one would see her.

The king's wagon went back to the palace. A servant took the apples off the wagon and found the girl. The servant was kind and helpful. He let her stay and work at the palace in the kitchen.

The king had a handsome son. He was very kind to people. He also liked to help in the kitchen.

The next day he met the new servant girl. He listened to her story, and they fell in love. When the old king died, the son became king. He was a kind ruler and did not take the best apples from the poor, and the people loved him.

STORY QUESTIONS

1. What word best describes the servant?
   a. unhelpful
   b. kind
   c. mean
   d. nasty

2. The old king was . . .
   a. loving.   c. mean.
   b. kind.   d. caring.

3. How was the son different than the old king?
   a. He was kind.
   b. He wanted bananas instead of apples.
   c. He lived in the palace.

DAILY Warm-Up 13

Name _____ Date _____

WHY BEES BUZZ

"Why do bees buzz, Grandfather?" asked the boy.

"I will tell you a story," said the old man. "It is a sad story."

"Tell me, Grandfather. Tell me now."

"A long time ago, people and bees were friends. They talked, played, and they sang. They danced under the moon. The bees loved the people, and the people loved the bees."

"Go on, Grandfather," said the boy.

"One day it was dark outside. The sun did not come up in the sky. No one could see to turn on the lights. No one could make food, and no one could start a fire."

"Then what?"

"A bee was sleeping in his bed. A little boy went looking for a light and then hit the bee on the head because the boy could not see. The bee got a bad bump on his head. The boy tried to say he was sorry, but the bee did not listen and just buzzed instead of talking."

"But why did the bee stay mad?"

"He did not want to listen to the boy. He told all the other bees to buzz and not talk to people. Now bees and people are not friends anymore. Now they do not talk. They just buzz."

STORY QUESTIONS

1. What happened to the bee?
   a. He went to the zoo.
   b. He fell off his bike.
   c. He got a gift.
   d. He got a bump on the head.

2. How did the bee bump his head?
   a. He was chasing a mouse.   c. A boy hit him.
   b. The bee fell off his bed.   d. The bee hit a tree.

3. What folklore story is this like?
   a. "Little Red Hen"   c. "Snow White"
   b. "Little Red Riding Hood" d. "Why Mosquitoes Buzz in People's Ears"

DAILY
Warm-Up 14

Name _____ Date _____

KARL AND THE TALKING KIWI

Karl was a bad ant. He lived in a kiwi patch. The kiwi plants were big, and Karl was tiny. Karl made holes in the kiwis so he could play and take naps inside of them.

One night he saw a big, black cat walk by the kiwi patch. It was Oscar, the cat.

Karl wanted to play a trick on Oscar. So Karl ran inside one of the big kiwis. It was dark. Karl yelled, "Hey, you ugly cat!"

Oscar stopped and looked around. "Who said that?"

"I did, you ugly cat."

Oscar looked again. "Who are you and why are you calling me ugly?"

"I am down here. I am a talking kiwi, you ugly cat!"

Oscar found the talking kiwi and wanted to show it to the king.

Karl did not say a word. The king asked the kiwi to talk, but it said nothing. The king kept asking it questions. The kiwi did not make a noise.

Oscar told the king it could talk, and he had talked to it earlier in the day.

The king got mad and threw it at the wall. The kiwi broke into many pieces. Karl fell out. The king was very mad when he saw the trick Karl had played on the cat. Karl had to work for the king and promise that he would not do any more tricks again.

"No more time for tricks! Only work and more work for you!" yelled the king.

STORY QUESTIONS

1. What kind of ant was Karl?
   a. He was nice ant.
   b. He was a bad ant.
   c. He was a cute ant.
   d. He was a fuzzy ant.

2. Where did Karl hide?
   a. in a kiwi
   b. in a tree
   c. in the cat's fur
   d. in the king's food

3. What did the king do to punish Karl?
   a. He made him eat lots of kiwis.
   b. He made him do lots of work.
   c. He made him say "Sorry!" to the cat.
   d. He did not do anything.

DAILY
Warm-Up 15

Name _____   Date _____

JUMPING JELLYFISH

Chad was a clam. One day he was taking a nap. He then opened one of his eyes. Do you know what he saw? He saw Jerry jumping outside his window. Jerry was a jellyfish.

"I wonder why Jerry Jellyfish is jumping," he said. "I had better jump too."

So Chad Clam went outside and started to jump.

Sammy was a Sea Star. He was finding things to eat when he saw Chad Clam and Jerry Jellyfish jumping.

"I wonder why they are jumping," Sammy Sea Star said to himself. "If Jerry Jellyfish and Chad Clam are jumping, I want to jump too."

Just then Sara Shark saw Jerry Jellyfish, Chad Clam, and Sammy Sea Star jumping. Sara Shark didn't know why they were jumping, but she just thought that she should join them. So Sara Shark jumped and jumped.

Wilber was swimming by, looking something to do. Wilbur was a great, big whale. He stopped by to say "hello" to all his friends.

"Hello, everybody! Why is everybody jumping?" said Wilber Whale

"I don't know," Sara Shark said. "Ask Jerry Jellyfish. He was jumping first."

"Jerry!" yelled Wilber. "Why are you and everybody else jumping?"

"Why are they jumping? I don't know. I am jumping to get my exercise!"

STORY QUESTIONS

1. What was Sammy Sea Star doing before he saw his friend jumping?
   a. He was finding something to eat.   c. He was playing in the plants.
   b. He was sleeping.   d. He was sitting on a rock.

2. Why was Jerry Jellyfish jumping?
   a. He just liked to jump up and down.   c. He was doing his exercises.
   b. He was a jellyfish.   d. He wanted people to look at him.

3. Why were all of the animals jumping?
   a. They all liked to jump.
   b. They were doing what Jerry was doing.
   c. They were jumping for a contest.
   d. They wanted to jump the highest.

DAILY
Warm-Up 16

Name _____ Date _____

LITTLE BLUE BONNET

A little girl named Ashley lived with her mom and dad. They lived on the top of a hill in a big house. It had five rooms.

Ashley loved to cook and bake. She loved to make biscuits, and she loved to make cookies. She loved to bake for her grandmother.

Every day she wore a little blue hat on her head. It was a bonnet. Wearing the bonnet, she made cookies and muffins for her grandmother.

The people in the town started to call her "Little Blue Bonnet."

One day she was late to grandmother's house to give her the baked goods. She ran into the woods to take a shortcut. She had a feeling that someone was following her. It was a wolf who wanted her cookies, and he wanted her muffins. He also wanted to eat her.

The wolf got to the grandmother's house before Little Blue Bonnet. He quickly put on the grandmother's clothes.

Little Blue Bonnet finally made it to her grandmother's house. She knocked on the door. The door slowly opened. Who do you think Little Blue Bonnet saw?

STORY QUESTIONS

1. Which parts are in the right order?
   a. She went to Grandma's. She cooked. She went to Grandma's.
   b. She lived with her parents. She cooked. She went to Grandma's.
   c. She cooked. She went to Grandma's. She ate the cookies.
   d. She saw the wolf. She went to Grandma's. She made cookies.

2. What did the wolf want from her?
   a. He wanted to smell the goodies.
   b. He wanted to make a new friend.
   c. He wanted to read a new book.
   d. He wanted to eat the goodies.

3. Whom do you think Little Blue Bonnet saw at the door?
   a. the wolf   c. her dad
   b. her mom   d. her grandmother

DAILY Warm-Up 1

Name _____   Date _____

SAM WALKS ON THE MOON

Sam loved to read books about space. He loved to look out at the moon at night. He loved to write stories about men in space. Sam drew pictures of the moon and space ships.

He knew about astronauts. Astronauts studied the stars. They studied space. They went there in space shuttles.

Sam went to bed. He was dreaming about space. He sat up in his bed. He looked all around.

He was not in his bed. He was wearing a white suit. He had a funny round hat on his head. He had gloves on his hands. He was wearing big boots on his feet.

"Hello," said Neil Armstrong. "Do you want to take a walk with me on the moon?"

"Yes!" said Sam. And he did.

STORY QUESTIONS

1. What did Sam like most of all?
a. space
b. math
c. reading
d. TV

2. What was Sam wearing in his dream?
a. mittens, blue suit, pink hat
b. a swimsuit and goggles
c. shorts and a shirt
d. a white suit, a funny round hat, gloves, and big boots

3. What do you think Neil Armstrong is?
a. a teacher   c. a doctor
b. an astronaut   d. a baker

Name _____   Date _____

"I HAVE A DREAM"

Cindy lived in Maine. She had black hair and brown eyes. She had lots of friends. All of her friends did not look the same. Cindy did not think about the color of their skin. She liked her friends because they were fun, and they were nice.

At school her teacher was talking about people. She said, "A long time ago people could not be friends if they were not the same color. They had to go to different schools. They could not eat at the same place. They could not drink out of the same water fountains. They could not go to the same schools."

Cindy was thinking hard. She started to dream.

A black man was standing on the steps of the Lincoln Memorial in Washington, D.C. He was talking. People were clapping. They were cheering. It was 1963. It was a hot day, and Cindy could feel the warm air.

She stepped closer. She heard him say, "I have a dream. It is a dream that all people can be kind to each other."

Cindy clapped and cheered. She smiled at the girl next to her. On the steps was Martin Luther King, Jr.

STORY QUESTIONS

1. Where is Cindy in her dream?
   a. in Maine
   b. on the steps of the Lincoln Memorial
   c. in her bed
   d. in her class at school

2. How does Cindy feel about the skin color of her friends?
   a. She thinks it is not important.
   b. She thinks it is important.
   c. She cares about it.
   d. She hates being the color that she is.

3. Who is the man on the steps of the Lincoln Memorial?
   a. Martin Luther King, Jr.
   b. George Washington
   c. Thomas Jefferson

A PILGRIM DAY

"Em, it's time for bed," called her mom.

Emily pulled the sheets over her head. She wanted to read for five more minutes. Emily waited until mom went to her room. She took out her flashlight and turned it on. The room started to move. It was going in circles.

She was wearing a dress. It had an apron on the front. She wore big shoes. They had buckles. Her bed was made out of straw.

"Emily, time to eat," called Ma.

She went down the ladder.

"Today is the day you have to do all the chores. I have to walk to go see Grandma Eliza."

"I know, Ma. In the morning I feed the hens. I get the eggs and sweep the floor. I have to watch baby Liz, too."

"And in the afternoon?"

"Set the table, first. Fix Pa his dinner. Wash the dishes and put them on the shelf. Before bed I have to write on my slate. Pa will help me with my letters and numbers."

"Today we will see how big you are! I am counting on you!"

"I will do all the chores, Ma. Take good care of Grandma. She needs you too."

STORY QUESTIONS

1. Why is Emily doing all the chores today?
   a. She wants to help out.
   b. She likes doing all of the chores.
   c. She wants to make money.
   d. Her mom is going to see Grandma Eliza.

2. Which chores does she have to do in the morning?
   a. feed the hens, get the eggs, sweep the floor, and watch Liz
   b. set the table, fix Pa his dinner, wash the dishes, put them on the shelf
   c. write on her slate, practice her letters and numbers

3. What word best describes Emily?
   a. lazy   b. busy   c. mean

Name _____ **Date** _____

ONE-ROOM SCHOOLHOUSE

Amos and Elizabeth were walking to school. There was a lot of snow. It was 1885. They lived in Walnut Grove. They walked one mile to school every day.

Amos was seven, and Elizabeth was 10. They were in the same class. All of the kids in the town were in the same class. There were 17 students. Their school only had one room. It was called a one-room schoolhouse.

Amos started a fire in the big stove. It kept them warm on cold days. Lizzie cleaned the desks. Some desks were big, and some were small. They all sat in rows.

Miss Laura put slates on all of the desks. She put chalk in the front of the room. Lizzie cleaned the board with a wet cloth. Miss Laura opened the book to the right page.

The bell rang for school to start. All the children came to school. They put their coats on the hooks in the hall. They put their lunches down by their desks. They took the snow off their boots. All of the students stood up to say the pledge to the flag.

The children then ate lunch and played games in the middle of the day. Some children played marbles. Others jumped rope and played clapping games. Some children ran races. Some played ball with sticks.

When the day was over, the children got their books and walked home.

STORY QUESTIONS

1. How many rooms are in the school?
   a. 1
   b. 3
   c. 4
   d. 2

2. Which **compound word** means "a place that is used to have school"?
   a. seashore   c. schoolhouse
   b. everyday   d. notebook

3. How is their school different from yours?
   a. They have one teacher for all of the grades.
   b. They had many teachers for each grade.
   c. They had many rooms in their school.

STARS IN HER EYES

Lexi is seven years old. She is in the first grade. She has long blond hair, and she has blue eyes. She always wants her mom to fix her hair in long curls. Lexi loves to go to the movies. It is 1935.

Today is Saturday. It is almost 10 A.M. Lexi is talking to her mom.

"Can we go to the movies today?"

"Maybe, Lexi. What do you want to see?" smiles her mother.

"I was thinking a movie with Shirley Temple would be good," they both said at the same time.

Lexi and her mom giggled.

Every Saturday they went to the movies. They went to see their favorite star. She was ten. Her hair was blond. It was curled in long rings. She could sing and dance. She had been a movie star since she was seven.

"Can we sing 'Good Ship Lollipop'?" asked Lexi.

"Sure," said Mom. "Let's grab our coats. It's time to go."

"On the good ship lollipop . . . ," sang Lexi and her mom. It would be a great day at the movies!

STORY QUESTIONS

1. What famous movie person does Lexi love?
   a. Shirley Temple
   b. Sandra Bullock
   c. Lizzie McGuire
   d. Denzel Washington

2. Where do Lexi and her mom go on Saturdays?
   a. to the bank
   b. to the store
   c. to the movies
   d. to the park

3. How are Shirley and Lexi like each other?
   a. They are both boys.
   b. They are both seven.
   c. They both have blond curly hair.

HENRY LEARNS TO FLY

Henry was lying down in the grass. He did not want anyone to see him. The grass was tall, so he was safe.

Two brothers were working not far away. They were making something that looked funny. It had two wheels. One was in the front. The other was in the back.

"Hey, Orville, could you help me with this?" asked Wilbur.

The boys worked and worked. They put something on top of the wheels. The boys got on, and it started to move. It went faster and faster.

Henry yelled, "What are you doing?"

"We are trying to fly," they said.

"Can I learn how to fly, too?" he asked.

"Maybe," they said.

Henry went home and asked his mother. She said, "<u>Yes</u>." Henry watched and waited. In 1903, they made something that had a motor, and it had wings. It was made of cloth. It was made of wood.

Orville got inside of it. Wilbur smiled. They started the engine. It moved into the air. It stayed in the air for 12 seconds.

Henry yelled, "Now, that is flying!"

STORY QUESTIONS

1. What did the boys want to do?
   a. dance
   b. swim
   c. ride
   d. fly

2. An **antonym** is a word that means the opposite. The antonym for *yes* is . . .
   a. all right.   c. for sure.
   b. okay.   d. no.

3. How long did they get the plane to fly?
   a. 12 seconds
   b. 21 seconds
   c. 22 seconds

DAILY
Warm-Up 7

Name _____ Date _____

GRANDPA AND THE FIVE AND DIME

Little Kip snuggled up in Grandpa Allen's lap. "Tell me a story," he said.

"What kind of story?" asked Grandpa.

"I want to hear a story about the five and dime store," Kip said. "I want you to tell me about how you met Grandma."

"All right," said Grandpa. "It was a long time ago—1923. I was 15. One day my dad left. My mom did not make lots of money. We had three boys to feed."

"So what did you do, Grandpa?"

"I did what I had to do. I got a job. "

"Were you old enough, Grandpa?"

"No. I had to tell them I was older. They gave me the job and I worked very hard. The store was called Woolworths. Everything was five or 10 cents."

"That's not a lot of money," said Kip.

"Not now, it isn't. But, at that time it was a lot of money. It was hard. There was a war. Not many people had money for extra things."

"So, what about Grandma?"

"Well, one day we got a new clerk. She was very pretty. She was nice. I liked her right away. I could not ask her on a date. We could not date people at our jobs."

"So what did you do?"

"I asked her to marry me. She said, "Yes." She had to get a new job and we got married on a weekend."

"Were you glad, Grandpa?"

"Oh, yes. Very glad."

STORY QUESTIONS

1. How much did things cost at Woolworth's store?
a. 6 or 7 cents
c. 5 or 15 cents
b. 5 or 10 cents
d. 10 or 20 cents

2. The **compound word** that means "all of the things" is . . .
a. nothing.
c. everything.
b. something.
d. weekend.

3. Tell what kind of sentence this is: Were you glad, Grandpa?
a. exclamatory
b. declarative
c. interrogative

Name _____ **Date** _____

CRAYONS

In 1885, two men had an idea. They wanted to make things to sell. They wanted to sell ink. They wanted to sell polish for shoes.

Their names were Edwin and C. Harold. They were cousins. They paid money for an old building. It gave them a new idea. Why not make slates for kids to use at school? All kids needed to write. They wanted to make things to help kids write. They made a wax marking stick that was black. It was not good for kids. It was too strong. They tried and tried again. In 1903, they had a new idea.

Edwin's wife had an idea. "Why don't you mix the wax with charcoal? Can you make other colors? I think children would like to use other colors."

"I think we can," said Edwin. He and Harold went to work. Soon they had black, brown, blue, purple, orange, yellow, and green.

"I think we should call them crayons," said Alice.

"I like it," said Edwin. "It means chalk that is oily."

"Let's put them in a box," said Harold.

"I think we should sell them for five cents each," said Alice.

"You are a smart lady," said Edwin. "That is why I love you!"

STORY QUESTIONS

1. Why do you think kids like crayons so much?
   a. They are ugly.
   b. They are fun to color with.
   c. They make a big mess.
   d. They are fun to eat.

2. How did they decide to sell the crayons?
   a. in a suitcase
   b. in a bag
   c. in a box
   d. tie them with string

3. Who made the first crayons?
   a. Edwin and C. Harold
   b. Edwin and Alice
   c. Mark and Luke

BAND-AIDS

In 1920, Eva went over to her friend's house. She had made a fresh pie. Eva knocked on the door. Mrs. Dickson asked Eva to come in. She was baking, too. As she was cutting the apple, Mrs. Dickson cut her finger. It started to bleed. She put a wet cloth on the cut finger.

Eva put the pie on the table. She asked, "May I help you, Mrs. Dickson?"

"No, Eva. I am always cutting myself," she said. "My husband, Mr. Dickson has made a new kind of cloth just for me. I think I will put on one of the new cloths now."

"Where is the cloth?" asked Eva.

"It is over there in that small tin box. It says, 'Band-Aids' on it," she said.

"I found it," said Eva. Eva opened the box. She took out one of the Band-Aids®. Eva watched. Mrs. Dickson peeled off the back. She stuck the small cloth on her finger.

"That is much better," said Mrs. Dickson. "I think these cloths will work very well."

"Do you think he would make some for me?" asked Eva.

"I think he might," she said with a smile. "Why don't we ask him now!"

STORY QUESTIONS

1. What happened to Mrs. Dickson?
   a. She got in a fight with her friend.
   b. She burned the pie.
   c. She cut her finger.
   d. She made a stain on the cloth.

2. For whom did Mr. Dickson make the first Band-Aid?
   a. his mother
   c. his daughter
   b. his wife
   d. his son

3. Why do you think Band-Aids become so popular?
   a. People like to buy new things.
   b. People everywhere cut themselves.
   c. People like new colors.
   d. People think sticky things are cool.

DAILY Warm-Up 10   Name _____   Date _____

TOLL HOUSE COOKIES

In 1930, Tim and his family were staying at an inn for the night. The inn was called the Toll House Inn.

Mrs. Wakefield was baking cookies. She and Ken owned the inn.

Mrs. Wakefield asked Tim, "Would you like to help me make cookies?"

"Sure," said Tim. "What can I do?"

"You can mix the dough," she said.

"I am good at mixing. I help my mom all of the time."

"Oh, dear," she said. "I am out of baking chocolate. What will I do?"

Tim watched as Mrs. Wakefield took out a bar of chocolate. She cut it into little pieces.

"What are you going to do with that candy bar?" asked Tim.

"I am making it into chunks," she said.

"Why are you going to do that? Why not just eat the chocolate?" asked Tim.

"I am going to try something new. It will be a test. We will see how it turns out," she said.

"Okay," said Tim, as he mixed in the pieces.

Mrs. Wakefield put scoops of the cookie dough onto a cookie sheet. She put it into the oven to bake.

When the cookies came out, she looked surprised. "This is new."

Tim took a big bite. "Yummy!" said Tim. "What are these cookies called?"

"I think I will call them Toll House cookies," she said.

"That is a good name," said Tim. "I think I would like another Toll House cookie, please!"

STORY QUESTIONS

1. Why did Mrs. Wakefield use chocolate bars?
a. She wanted to make something new.
b. She ran out of baking chocolate.
c. She was in a hurry.
d. She didn't like baking chocolate any more.

2. Tell what kind of sentence this is: Yummy!
a. exclamatory   c. interrogative
b. declarative   d. none of these

3. When Mrs. Wakefield took the cookies out of the oven, what happened?
a. Everyone said they were nasty.   c. No one liked them at all.
b. Everyone said they were too soft.   d. Everyone liked them.

THE HORSELESS CARRIAGE

In 1896, Verland and his sister, Marie, lived in Detroit, Michigan. One day, they were playing marbles in front of their home.

Suddenly, Verland stood up, "Hey, Sis! Look! Look!"

Marie stood up and looked. She saw a funny-looking carriage rolling down the dirt road. It made a "putt-putt" noise.

"What is it?" she asked.

"I don't know," Verland said.

"How is it moving? Where are the horses?" asked Marie.

"I don't know," said Verland.

The carriage went past them slowly. It made a strange noise. "Putt. Putt. Putt." It was black and had four big wheels. A man was sitting inside. He was holding a big wheel in his hand. The strange thing stopped at the end of the street. The children ran all the way to the carriage.

"Hey, Mister! What are you riding in?" they asked.

"It's a horseless carriage," said the man.

"How does it move?" asked Marie.

"It moves with an engine, but does not use horses," said the man.

"Wow!" said the two children.

"Who made it?" they asked.

"I did," said the man.

"Who are you?" they asked.

"I am Henry Ford."

STORY QUESTIONS

1. What kind of person is Verland?
   a. a boy who sells ice cream
   b. a boy who does not like people
   c. a boy who asks a lot of questions
   d. a boy who cleans shoes

2. What do you think a horseless carriage was?
   a. a wagon with no horse
   b. a plane
   c. a boat
   d. a car

3. Which one is **NOT** a fact about Henry Ford?
   a. She is a girl.
   b. He made cars.
   c. His first name was Henry.

DAILY Warm-Up 12

Name _____ Date _____

LIFE SAVERS

Clarence Crane made chocolates. He had his own shop. It was 1912.

One day he was working. "I want to make candy that will not melt in the summer," he told his wife.

"That is a good idea," she said. "I think you should try to make a new kind of candy."

Clarence worked and worked. He mixed up white sugar. He added this. He added that. He put in a drop of peppermint.

"Let me taste," said his wife. She took a bite. "This is good. Why don't you put it into your machine? I will turn the handle."

"Let's see what it will look like," said Clarence. He put it in the machine. He turned the handle. It made a hole in the center of the white, sweet candy.

"It looks like a life preserver from the *Titanic*," said his wife.

"It is missing the red stripes," said Clarence.

"It is too small for a mouse!" she said. "But, it does look good. What will we call it?"

"I think we should call it a Life Saver™," he said. "<u>What do you think, dear?</u>"

"I think that is a good idea. It is time for me to have a Life Saver, don't you think?" she asked. He handed one to her and they both smiled.

STORY QUESTIONS

1. Who made the first Life Saver candy?
   a. Uncle Sam
   b. Clarence Crane
   c. George Washington
   d. Henry Ford

2. What did his wife think the candy looked like?
   a. a life preserver from the *Titanic*
   b. a wheel from a bike
   c. a ring
   d. a ball

3. Tell what kind of sentence this is: <u>What do you think, dear?</u>
   a. exclamatory
   b. declarative
   c. interrogative

Name _____ Date _____

A MODEL HOUSE

As a child, John Lloyd Wright liked to watch his dad. His dad, Frank Lloyd Wright, made models of houses. He made the models out of thin pieces of wood. He made them look like the real thing. He painted on the windows. He made doors that could open and shut.

John wanted to be like his dad. He wanted to make models of houses, too. John did not have things to use to make model houses. He did not know how he could make models like his dad.

When John turned 24 years old, he had an idea. He made a little set of logs. John used a sharp knife. They were very small. He could hold them in his hand. The logs were made from wood. They had little cuts in each of the ends. The logs could be stacked. They could be turned. They could be made into a house.

"I will call them Lincoln Logs™," he said. "I think many children will want to build houses with them."

His idea was a hit. Kids wanted to play with his Lincoln Logs. It was 1916.

STORY QUESTIONS

1. Why did John make Lincoln Logs?
   a. He wanted to take them to the zoo.
   b. He liked the color.
   c. He wanted to make models like his dad.
   d. He wanted his dad to be happy.

2. What is this story all about?
   a. The cat who hit a ball.
   b. The girl who jumped a log.
   c. The lady who swam a river.
   d. The man who invented Lincoln Logs for kids.

3. Which sentence is **NOT TRUE** about Lincoln Logs?
   a. They are very small.
   b. They are big and fat.
   c. You can hold them in your hands.
   d. They have little cuts near the ends.

DAILY
Warm-Up 14

Name _____ Date _____

THE MEAT PLANT

It was 1955. Lloyd was 19 years old. His best friend, Ken, was 19, too. They needed to get jobs. They needed to earn money.

They got a job in a meat plant. The meat plant was in Kansas. It was called Armour and Company.

Lloyd had to work on the line. His job was to take the bacon off the line. He had to put in under a big roller. The roller looked like a big rolling pin. It was as big as a tree stump. The roller pressed the meat and made it into bacon.

Lloyd also had to take the pork loins off the belt. He had to put them into a big metal chute. It looked like a slide from the park. It had a big mouth. It was six feet long. It had a hole at both ends. The meat went through the chute. It came out the other side.

Ken cut the fat off the meat. He had to do it by hand. He had to cut it with a sharp knife.

Other workers put the meat into boxes. They put it on trucks. The trucks took it to stores, and the stores sold it to the people.

It was cool in the plant. All the workers wore sweatshirts. It was like being in a big freezer. They all had jobs until the meat was all cut. When there were no more orders for meat, the plant closed down. It stayed closed until someone needed a lot of meat again.

STORY QUESTIONS

1. Why were Ken and Lloyd working at the meat plant?
   a. They liked to cut meat.
   b. They liked it because it was cold in the freezer.
   c. They likes to wear sweatshirts to work.
   d. They needed to make money.

2. Compound words are words are made up of two words that are put together to make a new word. Which compound word means "a shirt that is warmer than most of them"?
   a. overshirt   b. undershirt   c. sweatshirt

3. What was the chute for pork loins like?
   a. a big slide   b. a small slide   c. a swing set

DAILY
Warm-Up 15

Name _____

Date _____

IN THE MINE

Will and his friend were looking for work. They saw an ad in the paper. It said, "Good jobs! Good pay! Work in the mines of Montana! Apply today!"

Will and his friend called the mine. The mine said they had work if the boys wanted to work.

They each packed a small bag. They got into Will's car and drove to Montana.

Will got a job driving a train in the mine. Billy got a job loading sand.

Every night they started working at 6 P.M. They went down into the mine. They rode in a small box with no windows. Each boy brought a lunch. They each wore a helmet and a jacket.

Will had to work with Billy. Will drove the train. Billy put the sand on the cars that Will pulled with the engine.

Billy opened the chute and filled each car with sand.

Will drove the train to the spot that had been dug out. The ore was gone. The miners had sent it to the top of the mine. He poured the sand in the hole, and he added water.

He and Billy packed the sand. They packed it so the mine would not cave in. The sand would keep the city from sinking into the ground.

It was a cold job. The tunnels had no light. Will used the light on his helmet to see where to drive. Billy zipped up his jacket. They worked hard and fast.

Billy opened and closed the chute. He put sand in the cars. Will drove the train. All night they worked. When the sand was gone, it was time to go home for the night.

STORY QUESTIONS

1. What time did Will go to work?
a. 3 A.M.
b. 6 A.M.
c. 6 P.M.
d. 10 P.M.

2. What was Will's job?
a. loading the sand
b. driving the train
c. shoveling dirt
d. looking for lost miners

3. When did the Ken and Will get to go home from work?
a. when all of the sand was gone
b. when they wanted to
c. after they ate lunch

DAILY Warm-Up 16

Name _____ Date _____

ORE BOAT ON THE GREAT LAKES

It was the summer or 1953. George just got a job on a big boat. The boat ran on the Great Lakes. It went from Wisconsin to Ohio every three days. The boat took many things back and forth.

George and his friend, Petey, both got jobs on the ship.

"Hey, George, what job did you get?" asked Petey.

"The captain says I am to work as a deck hand," said George.

"I am going to work in the engine room," said Petey. "I think I would like it better outside. I am not sure I want to stay in a room with a lot of noise."

"It will be okay," said George. "We can read books when we get off work. They have a library. They have a mess hall too. The food looks very good. I think I want to eat five times a day."

"Good luck with that! I want to paint the ship and clean the deck. I want to tie the ship up when we get into port. I want to clean the hold of the ship," said Petey.

"You need to talk to the boss. I think you have the wrong job," said George. "Maybe we could trade."

"I think that would be great," said Petey. "I need the fresh sea air. I need to stretch my legs. You are good with engines, and you can fix anything that breaks. You are the man for the job!"

They laughed. It was time to talk to the captain and see if they could <u>swap</u> jobs.

STORY QUESTIONS

1. Why did the boys want to change jobs?
   a. They were too old to work.
   b. They wanted to jump in water.
   c. They wanted to talk to the boss.
   d. They both got jobs they did not want.

2. Synonyms are words that mean the same thing. *Swap* is a synonym for the word . . .
   a. clean　　　　　b. do　　　　　c. exchange

3. Who was the best man for working in the engine room?
   a. George　　　　　b. Petey　　　　　c. the captain

DAILY Warm-Up 1

Name _____ Date _____

FRANK

"I just hate math," said Frank. "Do you like it, Sam?"

"I do," I said. "It is my best subject."

My real name is Samantha J. Bruger. I am sitting by Frank. I don't think it will be fun. I think he will bug me. We are in the first grade, room 21. It is my first day at a new school. My family just moved here from another state. My dad got a new job, and we have to go to a new school.

"Take out your pencil," Frank said. "It is time for math."

"It is already on my desk. See?"

He looked at my desk. I was ready. The math book was propped open and the answers were already done.

"Wow," said Frank. "When did you do that?"

"Just now. It only took two minutes."

Frank raised his hand. "Ms. Smith, do you think I can sit by Sam all year?"

"I don't know, Frank. A year is a long time. Why do you ask?"

"Well, I think she is real good at math. If I sit by her some of that 'goodness in math' might rub off on me!"

I giggled. The teacher giggled. We all giggled. Maybe sitting by Frank wouldn't be so bad after all.

STORY QUESTIONS

1. "The math book was propped open" means . . .
   a. it was held open with something.   c. it was flipping the pages.
   b. it was going closed.   d. it was in the middle of the story.

2. What sentence might be **TRUE** about Frank?
   a. He wanted to bug Samantha.
   b. He was trying to be a pest.
   c. He was trying to help in his own way.
   d. He wanted Samantha to play tetherball

3. What do you think will happen next?
   a. Frank will bug Sam every day.   c. Frank will not like Sam at all.
   b. They will become friends.

DAILY
Warm-Up 2

Name _____ Date _____

YUCKY

"School is yucky. Recess is yucky. Teachers are yucky. Today is yucky!" yelled Rachel. She sat down on the playground and started to cry.

"What is wrong, Rachel?" asked Payton. "Why are you crying?"

"Go away. Leave me alone."

"But, Rachel, I am your friend."

"Go away! I don't want to talk to anybody now. It is a bad day!"

"I am your friend. I will not go away. I will sit with you in the dirt. I will listen to your stories. I will cry with you."

Rachel stood up, "Go away! I do not want any friends. I want to cry! I want to be sad! I want to punch my brother!"

"Why do you want to punch your brother?" asked Payton.

"He put my homework in the dog dish last night. The dogs ate it. They ate all of my spelling words. The only word left was *from.*"

Payton started to laugh. She started to giggle. Her lips were moving and bubbles were coming out of her mouth.

"What is so funny?" asked Rachel.

Payton laughed, "I guess the dogs needed those words more than you did! What a tasty treat!"

STORY QUESTIONS

1. We can make a guess that Rachel was having a _____.
   a. mean teacher   c. bad day
   b. bad lunch   d. bad test

2. What **compound word** from the story means "a place to play"?
   a. playground   c. cupboard
   b. snowboard   d. outside

3. Which one is **NOT** a fact about Rachel?
   a. She wants to punch her brother.
   b. The dog ate her spelling words.
   c. She does not have her homework.
   d. She is having a good day.

DAILY Warm-Up 3

Name _____ Date _____

HOOPS

"Give me the ball!" yelled Hector. "Now! I want to shoot the hoops."

Manual threw the ball to Hector, "Catch!"

Hector took the ball and dribbled down the court.

He was getting closer to the basket. He knew he could make it.

"Shoot! Shoot!" yelled Pedro.

Hector shot. Anthony put his hand in front of the ball. It did not go into the basket. The other team got the ball. They ran down to the basket. They shot. It went in. Two points for the other team.

Manual got the ball. He passed to Hector. Hector passed to Pedro. Swish! It made it right in the basket.

The two teams threw the ball back and forth. Each team made a basket.

Swish! 2–2. 4–4. 8–6.

It was only one minute until recess was over. Hector's team was behind by two points. The boys ran down the court.

"Pass! Now!" yelled Hector.

Manual grabbed the ball. He tossed it with all his might. Swoosh! Right in the basket.

Brrrrrrrrrrrrrr. There goes the bell!

"Tie game!" they all yelled. "We'll play again at lunch."

STORY QUESTIONS

1. What game do you think the boys were playing at recess?
   a. soccer
   b. basketball
   c. tetherball
   d. baseball

2. What was the score with one minute left of recess?
   a. 2–2
   b. 10–10
   c. 8–6
   d. 4–4

3. What happened at the bell?
   a. The game was tied.
   b. Hector's team won.
   c. Anthony's team won.

DAILY
Warm-Up 4

Name _____ Date _____

THE BIG GAME

Coach R was the best coach. His hair was thin. He always wore his "best coach" jacket. We never saw him without it. He wore his blue sweat pants and his white shoes. He never got mad at us. He just looked funny if we did something wrong. His face would get red. He would put his board in his bag.

"Girls, it is all about the basics—just the basics. We win as a team, we lose as a team."

We all smiled. Before every game he said the same thing. "Remember the basics."

When we were on the field, we had to do what he said. Trap. Control. Pass. Dribble. Shoot. That is the way he wanted it done.

Today was no different. We all wanted to win. It was the last game of the year. Our team wanted the trophy. If not the trophy, we wanted the medals. It was our day. The prize was for us to have.

The sun was shining. We were getting hot. We gave our mittens to our moms and dads. Our team went on the field to play soccer.

"Trap. Control. Pass. Dribble. Shoot. Shoot. Shoot."

We shot. We scored. Our team listened to Coach R and we won. It was a great day. He is the best coach a team could have!

STORY QUESTIONS

1. What does Coach R always say before every game?
   a. "Trap. Control."
   b. "Control. Pass."
   c. "Remember the basics."
   d. "Pass. Dribble. Shoot."

2. How did the girls feel about their coach?
   a. They thought he was the best.
   b. They did not like him.
   c. They thought he was funny.
   d. They thought he was mean.

3. The girls are playing a game called . . .
   a. tetherball.
   b. baseball.
   c. soccer.

DAILY Warm-Up 5

Name _____ Date _____

MISSING MONEY

"Where is my lunch money?" <u>sobbed</u> Bill. "I just had it in my pocket."

His teacher heard him crying. "Where do you think you lost it?"

"I think I dropped it when I got out of the car."

"Do you want to go back out and look?"

"Yes, but I don't want to go alone."

"Go. Take Peter with you. Both of you can look on the sidewalk on the way to the parking lot."

They walked with their heads down. There was no money on the sidewalk.

No quarter was in the parking lot.

"Hey, Bill, look! I found two pennies."

"You can keep those. Nobody can get lunch with two pennies."

The two boys went to the office. They talked to the secretary.

"How much money did you lose?" she asked.

"I lost 25 cents," said Bill. He wasn't crying any more.

"I think this might be your lucky day. I think this belongs to you! A little boy came into the office. He found one quarter by the cars. He wanted to make sure I kept it safe."

"Really? Thanks, Ms. Nancy!"

Both boys ran back to the classroom. Bill had his money. He could eat lunch.

STORY QUESTIONS

1. Bill's lunch money was . . .
   a. in the office.
   b. in his backpack.
   c. in his desk.
   d. under his bed.

2. Which **compound word** from the story means "a place that kids go to have school"?
   a. bedroom
   b. inside
   c. classroom
   d. outside

3. **Synonyms** are words that mean the same thing. *Sobbed* is a synonym for what word?
   a. sang   b. cried   c. played

DAILY Warm-Up 6

Name _____ Date _____

PARTY

My name is Chris. Today is my birthday. I am eight years old. My mom is planning a party after school. We will have blue balloons and blue ice cream. All of the games have blue prizes, and I want to get a blue bike with shiny handles.

The day is going slowly. I keep watching the clock. It is only 9:00 A.M. That is when we have math. I love math. It makes me think of my birthday. Two dollars, plus four dollars, plus six dollars is twelve dollars. I will get that much money from my sisters. Three balloons and seven balloons make ten balloons. There are thirteen balloons in all. Six party hats and . . . .

"Chris, can you come to the board and do the math problem?"

"What did you say, Miss D? Are you talking to me?"

"Yes, Chris, I wanted you to add the numbers on the board?"

"Do they have chocolate cake or games? Do they have balloons or bikes?"

"Chris, what are you talking about? I want you to add six and eleven on the board."

"I'm sorry, Miss D. I guess I was thinking about my birthday. It is today."

"Right, Chris. We remembered. Your mom is bringing cake at 3:00. Remember?"

"I remember."

"Guess it is time to get back to math. What do you think, Chris?"

"I think you are right. I can think about the party later!"

STORY QUESTIONS

1. What was Chris thinking about all day at school?

    a. his dog   c. his party

    b. his cat   d. his chicken

2. Which is **NOT** something the class was doing?

    a. adding numbers on the board   c. learning to add

    b. doing math   d. selling pies

3. How is Chris like most kids in this story?

    a. When they are having a party, it is hard to think about other things.

    b. They all go to school on the weekends.

    c. They like to eat pizza.

DAILY
Warm-Up 7

Name _____ Date _____

SKIING

Have you ever gone to the mountains? Have you even felt the wind in your hair? I have. It feels nice when the wind blows in my ears. The wind makes a soft noise. My ears feel cold.

We go to Big Bear Mountain. My family likes to ski. We all rent skis at the lodge. I get size 3 boots. They are black. My dad helps me with the buckles. He pushes them down tight.

I carry my skis. They are short and shiny. It is hard to carry them, because they are almost as big as I am. I put them on when I get outside. The poles stand alone in the snow. The boots make a snapping sound when I put my feet into them. The snap means they are on. It means they are ready to go.

Next, I head up to the ski lift. We ride to the top of the small mountain. My dad and I race to the bottom. He is very fast. Dad doesn't even use his poles.

We go up and down. My mom and I ski together. Dad and I ski together. I ski with my sisters. The wind blows in my hair.

When the sun goes down, we are tired. Dad and I go to take off our skis. My sister turns in her snowboard. We all put on our boots. Our feet smell. Time to go home and rest.

STORY QUESTIONS

1. In what person is the author writing this story?
   a. third person
   b. second person
   c. first person
   d. last person

2. What do you think the family will do next?
   a. Eat sandwiches in the snow.
   b. Ski in the dark.
   c. Go to the snack bar.
   d. Go home and rest.

3. "The wind blows in my hair" probably means . . .
   a. the writer can feel the breeze on his head.
   b. the wind is his friend.
   c. the wind is playing a game.
   d. the wind is trying to make him mad.

DAILY Warm-Up 8

Name _____ Date _____

AFTER SCHOOL

"Can we go to the park?" I asked my mom. "Can we go after school?"

"We can," she said. "Don't forget to bring your skates."

"I won't," I promised. Skating is the thing I like best about the park.

All day long I think about the park. I dream. I plan. I am hoping I will see my friend. The day seemed so long.

"Hurry up, day!" I hear myself say. "Hurry up and get to 3:00. I want to go to the park."

My mother is waiting after school. My sisters and I hop into the car. We are happy. We all love the park.

"Guess what?" Mom asks.

"What?" we all say at the same time.

"I stopped and got us a bucket of chicken."

"Yes!" we shouted. "Did you remember the biscuits?"

"The biscuits, yes. The cold slaw, yes. The macaroni, yes. I have them all."

"Mom, you are the greatest!" we cried.

"Well, munchkins. I don't know about that, but I want to get to the park. I can hear my skates calling my name. Let's go!"

"We are with you, Mom. Drive on!"

STORY QUESTIONS

1. Where is the family going after school?
  a. to the zoo
  b. to the park
  c. to get fast food
  d. to the store

2. Which thing is **NOT** something the children like in this story?
  a. chicken
  b. skating
  c. biking
  d. biscuits

3. What is the best thing about the park?
  a. skating
  b. eating
  c. walking
  d. swinging

DAILY Warm-Up 9

Name _____ Date _____

FIGHT

"Fight! Fight! Fight!" yelled the kids.

The playground looked like ants running everywhere.

Two boys were in the center fighting. They were punching each other. They were throwing fists. Both boys were saying bad words and calling each other bad names.

It did not look good. I did not want to get in the middle of that fight. A boy pushed me as I stood on the circle. I fell into one of the boys that were fighting. He punched me in the head.

"That hurt!" I yelled. "Stop it! I do not want to fight with you. Let go of me!"

Now both boys were punching me. One hit my head. The other punched me in the tummy. It was not a good day at all. I did not want to fight. <u>Why was I in the middle of a war?</u>

Mr. Jones came out of the lunchroom. He opened the door and gave the "dirty look." We all stopped. I stared. My arms had bruises on them. The kids were all pointing to me. It was a nightmare,

Lucky for me, my mom came to wake me up in a few minutes. She pulled my pillow and touched my nose. I was still asleep when I said, "Do not punch me again. I might get a bloody nose!"

STORY QUESTIONS

1. Tell what kind of sentence this is: <u>Why was I in the middle of a war?</u>
   - a. both b and c
   - b. exclamatory
   - c. declarative
   - d. interrogative

2. We know that the fight was not real. It was a . . .
   - a. dream.
   - b. play.
   - c. party.
   - d. school day.

3. When the boys started punching the writer, he said, . . .
   - a. "Go and fight with another one your size!"
   - b. "Let go of me, you ape!"
   - c. "Stop it! I do not want to fight with you. Let go of me!"

DAILY Warm-Up 10

Name _____ Date _____

MY HAIR

When I woke up, I could feel it was going to be a bad day.

I looked in the mirror. My hair was standing up. It looked like a tree.

I screamed, "Mom, I look like a tree."

She said, "That's nice, dear. Please get ready for school."

I yelled, "Mom, my hair is sticking up on my head."

"That's nice, dear. Please, put on your clothes."

I could see waves all over my head. It looked like the ocean.

"Mom!"

"What!"

"I need help. My hair is a mess. I can't go to school like this. All of my friends will laugh at me."

"That's nice, dear. Please, eat your toast."

I walked down to the kitchen. Mom looked at me. "What is wrong with your hair?"

"I don't know," I said. "I guess it is a bad hair day."

"I guess so," said my mother.

Dad looked up from the paper and laughed. "Who cares if it is a bad hair day? You are both silly. Today is Saturday!"

STORY QUESTIONS

1. Why do you think the author was worried about his hair?
  a. He had to give a report at school.
  b. He thought it was a school day.
  c. He wanted to go to the park with his friends.
  d. He was going with Grandpa to the zoo.

2. What did the author's hair look like?
  a. a house   c. a car
  b. a tree   d. a truck

3. Dad was laughing because . . .
  a. he was telling good jokes.   c. he liked the hair.
  b. he was hungry.   d. it was Saturday.

NO HOMEWORK

My name is Carol Ann G. My friends called me "Cee" for short. I like the name. It works for me. I want to be a reporter when I grow up. This is my story.

It was the day before vacation. We were all very happy about that. Our class had talked about vacation. We talked about the things we wanted to do. We talked about where we wanted to go. We talked about what we would see.

It was just fine until Kirk stood up. He wanted a turn to talk. I don't like him much. He is always bossy and mean. Kirk always hits other kids at recess. He is never friendly.

"I will be going to Florida," Kirk said. "I will go to the beach and make sandcastles. My sister and I will play in the sand. We will buy hot dogs. The sun will be hot, and we will visit water parks."

"Thank you, Kirk," said my teacher. "That sounds like fun."

We all felt bad. Our ideas were not like Kirk's. We were not going to water parks. We would not go to the beach. This was Minnesota. It was cold. Snow was everywhere. We would read books. We would walk in the white snow. We would make snow angels.

The bell rang to end class. Our teacher stood up. She said, "We will all do different things on vacation. We will all see different things. The best part, I think, is that we will have no homework!"

We cheered! She was right. We smiled and went home happy.

STORY QUESTIONS

1. Why was the class happy at the end of the day?
   a. It was vacation, and they had no homework.
   b. They were going to a party.
   c. They were going skiing.
   d. They were giving food to the poor.

2. What does Carol want to be when she grows up?
   a. a builder   c. a reporter
   b. a carpenter   d. a brick layers

3. How does Carol describe Kirk?
   a. nice   c. mad
   b. mean

DAILY Warm-Up 12

Name _____ Date _____

BEST FRIENDS

I am Josh. My best friend is Joey, and we always play together. We walk to school together. We play at recess. He hits the ball first, and then I hit the ball second. Sometimes we take turns. We share our lunches. Joey gives me a snack, and I give him a snack. We tell secrets. We find frogs together. We play soccer in my backyard. We call each other on the phone. Joey and I tell jokes, and we laugh.

Today Joey said he was moving away. His dad got a new job, and they have to live in another place.

I went home mad. I kicked the door. I hit the mailbox. I ripped up my homework.

"What is wrong?" Mom asked.

"Joey is moving away," I said.

"You can write letters," said Mom.

"That is not good. I don't like writing letters."

"You can call him on the phone," said Mom.

"It is not the same as seeing him every day," I said.

"You can make new friends. There is a new boy just up the street. His mother said he is looking for a friend. They just moved in."

"I do not want a new friend. I want Joey," I said.

Just then the new boy rode his bike on the street. He waved, and I waved back.

"Maybe you will have a new friend after all," said Mom. I smiled.

STORY QUESTIONS

1. Who are best friends?
   a. Josh and Joey
   b. Josh and Henry
   c. Joey and Franky
   d. Pat and Ken

2. What do you think will happen next?
   a. Josh will go home and cry.
   b. Josh will go to camp.
   c. Josh will call Joey.
   d. Josh will make a new friend.

3. Which of these is **NOT** a fact from the story?
   a. A new boy just moved in on Josh's street.
   b. Joey has to move away.
   c. Joey and Josh are not friends.

THE BIG "D"

I am so happy today. My mom said that we are going for the big "D" tomorrow. I asked her what the big "D" was. She said the big drive to Grammy's house. Mommy says that we will stay there for a few days.

Daddy will have to stay home. He is very busy at work and cannot go. He will have to work late. He will have to cook his own dinner too. He will also have to make his own lunches.

Daddy read me a story at night. He kissed me. Dad said he would miss me very much. I started to cry. It is okay to cry, he says.

My mom packed my best red shirt. I got it for Christmas. I also wanted to take my blue pants and a picture of my daddy.

I know that time will go fast. I know I will see my daddy soon. My Grammy will fix me a pie to make me feel better. There will be lots of fun things to do. I will help Grammy with her garden. I will sit and swing with Grammy.

I can't wait to go to Grammy's house!

STORY QUESTIONS

1. What does the letter **D** stand for?
   a. dance
   b. dog
   c. donut
   d. drive

2. How does the author feel about the drive?
   a. He or she does not want to go.
   b. He or she wants to go to the zoo with Dad.
   c. He or she is very happy.
   d. He or she is mad and wants to cry.

3. What will the author's dad do while they are gone?
   a. cook his own food
   b. work late
   c. make his own lunch
   d. all of these

DAILY
Warm-Up 14

Name _____ Date _____

MOVING DAY

"Do you have your doll, Kali?" asked my dad.

"Yes, Dad," said Kali.

"Andy, put the dog in the truck," said dad.

"Okay, Dad."

"Mom, are you ready to go? We have to get going. Did you pack a lunch?"

"I did. I made tuna sandwiches with cheese."

"Yes!" we yelled. "Tuna with cheese!"

"Don't spill them in my new truck," said Dad.

We all hopped into the new, black truck. It was shiny. The engine was loud. Dad and Mom hopped in. We closed the doors, and Dad started the truck.

"I love this truck," said Andy.

"Me, too," I said. "It has a nice ride."

Mom turned on the radio. We all started to sing loudly.

"Hi, Ho, Hi, Ho, it's off to a new town we go."

Mom giggled. Dad laughed.

I stopped singing. "Dad, are you scared?"

"I guess I am, just a little bit. Why do you ask?"

"Well, I am a little scared. I am excited, too. Is that okay?"

"It is, princess. As long as we have each other, we will be fine!"

"Hi, Ho, Hi, Ho, it's off to a new town we go," we all sang.

STORY QUESTIONS

1. What song did the family sing to help them not be scared?
   a. "Hi, Ho, Hi, Ho, it's off to the zoo we go."
   b. "Hi, Ho, Hi, Ho, it's off to a new town we go."
   c. "Hi, Ho, Hi, Ho, it's off to the grocery store we go."
   d. "Hi, Ho, Hi, Ho, it's off to the water park we go."

2. What words from the story mean the same as the family "having butterflies in their stomachs"?
   a. They are all a little scared of moving.
   b. They all want to get going in the car.
   c. They are singing loudly in the truck.
   d. They are calling grandma.

3. How does the family feel about the truck?
   a. It is too small.   b. It is too shiny.   c. It has a nice ride.

DAILY
Warm-Up 15

Name _____ Date _____

STUCK IN THE SNOW FORT

It was a snowy day. The bell rang for recess and all of the kids ran to put on their boots.

"Remember to wear your hats. Remember your mittens. Remember to zip your coat. It is cold out today," said Mrs. M. Mrs. M was Tye's first grade teacher, and he liked her.

Tye was in a hurry to get outside. He was meeting his cousin, Cameron, at the snow fort. They had planned to make snowballs. The snow was wet and sticky. It was a great day.

"Hey, Tye, what took so long?" asked Cameron.

"I was putting on my coat. The zipper got stuck. Mrs. M helped me. She is a nice."

"Let's go. We need to hurry. I want to make snowballs."

The two boys ran to the fort. It was empty. They started to make snowballs. They put the balls inside.

Bam! Tye got hit with a snowball in the head. "Who threw that?"

"I don't know. We had better get inside quick," said Cameron.

They dived into the fort. Snowballs came in the windows. They came in the doors. Cameron peeked out. "It's Sara and Anna!" he yelled. "Get them, Tye!"

Both boys grabbed a snowball. They were stuck in the fort.

"Too bad, boys! You may only come out if you kiss us!" yelled the girls.

STORY QUESTIONS

1. Why were the boys stuck in the snow fort?
   a. The girls were trying to get them.   c. The door was closed.
   b. The ice had fallen in.   d. Snowballs filled the doorway up.

2. Which **compound word** means "balls made out of snow"?
   a. snowshoes   c. inside
   b. outside   d. snowballs

3. What do you think will happen next?
   a. The snow fort will fall down.
   b. The bell will ring, and the boys will get out.
   c. Cats and dogs will save the boys.

DAILY
Warm-Up 16

Name _____ Date _____

THE TENT

Jessica and Shelley were staying in the tent. The tent was in the yard. It was a nice night. There were stars in the sky. The moon was shining.

Jessica was telling Shelley stories. Shelley was pushing her toes in the bottom of her bag. Jessica was holding her bear.

A big bird flew over the tent, and a mouse ran by. The trees were moving in the wind. There was a noise on the side of the tent.

"It was a dark, starry night when Betsy Ross was sewing the flag . . . ," said Jessica.

Shelley wanted to scare Jessica so she thought of a plan.

"Can I tell a story?" Shelley asked.

"Yes," said Jessica. "It is your turn anyway."

Shelley took her light. Shelley moved the light under the blanket. When Jessica wasn't looking, Shelley threw her shoe against the wall. It made a loud noise.

"What was that?" asked Jessica.

"I think it was a big bug," said Shelley. "I think it wants to eat us!"

"How do you know?" asked Jessica.

"I saw it! It was huge!" Shelley <u>yelled</u>. Then Jessica yelled. Shelley said, "It was my old shoe! Got you!"

STORY QUESTIONS

1. What guess can we make about Shelley?
   a. Shelley wanted to hurt Jessica.
   b. Shelley liked to play tricks on people.
   c. Shelley liked big bugs.
   d. Shelley wanted to be brave.

2. Synonyms are words that mean the same thing. *Yelled* is a synonym for . . .
   a. talked   c. screamed
   b. whispered   d. said

3. Compound words are two words put together. Which compound word could be added to this story?
   a. grapefruit   b. backyard   c. lunchroom

DAILY Warm-Up 1

Name _____ Date _____

LIGHTS IN THE SHED

Last night I woke up at 10:00. There were lights outside my window. They were moving in my dad's shed. The lights kept moving up and down.

I was scared. I put my head under the covers. I went under the bed.

At 10:20, the lights were still there. They were bobbing up and down. The lights went on and off. Who was in my dad's shed?

It was time to read a book. The book was not scary. It was funny. It did not make me laugh.

I got up and went to the window. The lights were still moving. They were still bobbing up and down. I did not like it at all.

It was time to go down the hall. My parents would know what to do.

"Mom," I said when I came to her room. "Mom."

"What is it, dear?" she asked.

"Mom, there is someone in Dad's shed," I said.

"What?" she asked.

"There is someone in Dad's shed," I said.

"That is good," she said. "It is Dad. He is trying to catch the mouse!"

"Oh," I said. "I am going back to bed."

STORY QUESTIONS

1. Why did the author get scared?
   a. He fell on the chair.
   b. The bed moved.
   c. There were lights in the shed.
   d. He heard a noise in his room.

2. To whom did the author go for help?
   a. his friend
   b. his neighbor
   c. his dog
   d. his parents

3. What was the person doing in the shed?
   a. catching a mouse
   b. eating a cookie
   c. drinking milk
   d. playing a game

DAILY Warm-Up 2

Name _____

Date _____

THE BUS

"Beat you to the bus!" yelled Michael.

"No, you won't!" screamed Brad.

Both boys ran and ran. Their hair was flying through the air. They had their homework in their hands.

Michael dropped his papers.

Brad dropped his books.

"I will still win!" screamed Michael.

"I will win!" yelled Brad.

The boys picked up their things and ran.

Michael fell over a rock. "That dumb rock!" he yelled.

Brad fell on a bush. "Where did that bush come from?" asked Brad.

The boys got up. The boys ran.

The bus driver was yelling, "Hurry, boys! We will be late for school!"

Michael ran his fastest. Brad ran, too.

"Tie!" yelled the driver. "You'd better tie your shoes, too!"

STORY QUESTIONS

1. Who won the race?
   a. Michael
   b. Michael and Brad
   c. Brad
   d. the bus driver

2. Why do you think the boys were running to the bus?
   a. They were going to see the driver.
   b. They were going to the park.
   c. They were going to school.
   d. They wanted to win the prize.

3. Which sentence is **NOT** a fact about this story?
   a. Michael dropped his papers.
   b. Michael won the race.
   c. Brad dropped his books.
   d. The bus driver yelled, "Tie!"

DAILY Warm-Up 3

Name _____ Date _____

SNAPSHOT

Snap went the camera. Snap. Snap. Snap.

Kayla was visiting her grandma's farm. She was taking pictures to enter in the fair.

Snap. She took a picture of a fat, white lamb.

Snap. She took one of a big, black cow.

Snap. Snap. Snap. She wanted to take a picture of all of the animals on the farm.

"How are you doing?" asked Grandma.

"Just great," she said. "I think some of these pictures will win at the fair."

"Did you think about taking pictures of other things on a farm?" asked Grandma.

"Like what?" she asked.

"How about a big, fat spider?"

"Yuck," she said. "Why a spider?"

"They live here, too," said Grandma. "You may not think of it, but spiders are found on every farm in the world."

"I didn't think of that," said Kayla. "A picture of a spider would be good to have. I bet not everyone has thought of that."

"Probably not," said Grandma. "I know where there is a big, fat black one. Do you want to see it?"

"I do," said Kayla. "I want to win!"

STORY QUESTIONS

1. Why was Kayla taking pictures?
   a. She was starting a photo album.
   b. She liked to take pictures.
   c. She wanted to enter them in the fair.
   d. She was taking pictures for school.

2. What animal do you think Kayla will take a picture of next?
   a. a spider
   b. a sheep
   c. a chicken
   d. a cow

3. Where is the most likely place the big, black spider might be?
   a. on the moon
   b. in the park
   c. in the barn
   d. in the car

DAILY Warm-Up 4

Name _____ Date _____

THAT'S MY DOG!

"Thumper," I called. "Thumper, where are you?"

Our family just came home. We had been away for one week.

"Thumper," I called. "Thumper, we are home," I called.

Mom looked for Thumper. Dad looked for Thumper. He wasn't around.

"Thumper," we called.

"I think he is missing," I said.

We looked in the garage. We looked in the doghouse. No Thumper. He was not at the house.

We went in the house. We unpacked our bags. All I could do was think about Thumper. Was he hurt? Had he run away? Where was my dog?

I tried to unpack my bags. I tried to think about other things. My mind kept going back to Thumper. I started to cry.

I heard the phone ring. Dad was talking to someone. He was laughing.

"Teresa," Dad called. "Please come down here. Someone wants to talk to you!"

"Who is it, Dad?"

"You will see," he said with a smile.

I took the phone. "Hey, girl. It is Grandpa Allen."

"Hi, Grandpa, what's up?"

"I just called to tell you I came over last night. I hope you didn't mind. Thumper was sad. He was missing you. Grandma and I brought him home for the night. We left a note, but I think it blew away!"

STORY QUESTIONS

1. Why was the author worried about her dog?
   a. He was not there when they came home.
   b. He had a cut on his paw.
   c. He did not eat dinner.
   d. He did not wag his tail.

2. Who had Teresa's dog?
   a. her friend
   b. no one
   c. her grandpa
   d. the man next door

3. How are the little girl and Grandpa like each other in this story?
   a. They both drink coffee.
   b. They both love the dog.
   c. They both like football

DAILY Warm-Up 5 Name _____ Date _____

WHO'S AT MY HOUSE?

My dad and I were driving down the street. We stopped the car. We turned into the driveway.

"Who is that?" I asked.

"I do not know," said Dad. "He is in our house talking to your mom. She is waving at us."

We waved at Mom. We sat in the car and waited.

"Dad, what is going on?" I asked.

He looked at me.

I looked at him, "What is that man doing in our yard now?"

"I do not know," he said. "He looks very strange! He is wearing a mask."

We sat and waited. The man did not leave. He just talked to Mom. They were laughing. He was happy.

"Something is wrong," I said. "I will go and see."

"No, I will go and see," said Dad. He put his hands on his hips. He was not happy.

We walked to the house. The man turned around. He pulled off his mask. It was my Uncle Nate. He had come for a visit and was playing a trick on us.

"Hello, Dad. Hello, Ben! I am glad to see you!" said Uncle Nate.

"We are glad to see you, too!" we said. "What a nice surprise!"

STORY QUESTIONS

1. Why were dad and the boy scared when they came home?
   a. A man in their house had a banana.
   b. A man in their house had a gun.
   c. A man in their house was wearing a mask.
   d. A man in their house was in funny clothes.

2. Compound words are two words put together that make a new word. The compound word in this story that means "a place to drive" is . . .
   a. driveway.   c. streetcar.
   b. subway.   d. boxcar.

3. Who was wearing the mask?
   a. Uncle Kurt   c. Uncle Tim
   b. Uncle Kip   d. Uncle Nate

DAILY Warm-Up 6

Name _____ Date _____

CODES

"I want to be a secret agent," said A.L. "I want to write secret codes."

"Me, too," said S.B. "I think that would be cool."

We both wanted to be secret agents. Now was a good time to start. We were in first grade, Room 12.

My name is Ashley Lynne, and my best friend is Samantha Bean. We go by A.L. and S.B. for short.

Our teacher thinks we are very smart. We don't want to let her down, so we are going to show her what we can do. She says secret agents are smart, so we are going to be secret agents.

"I have a new code," I told S.B. at recess.

"I have one, too," she said.

We both took out our codes. I had made mine using letters. S.B. had made hers using pictures.

"I like them both, A.L.," she said. "I have an idea."

"What is it?" I asked.

"Why don't we use your code on Monday and Wednesday. We could use mine on Tuesday and Thursday. On Friday we could mix them and use them both."

"That sounds good to me," I said.

"Just remember," she said. "We must keep them out of enemy hands!"

STORY QUESTIONS

1. In what grade were Samantha Bean and Ashley Lynne?
   a. first
   b. second
   c. third
   d. fourth

2. Tell what kind of sentence this is: We must keep them out of enemy hands!
   a. interrogative
   b. declarative
   c. exclamatory
   d. none of these

3. Whose code do they use on Friday?
   a. Samantha's
   b. Ashley Lynne's
   c. both codes and mix them
   d. the teacher's

DAILY Warm-Up 7

Name _____ Date _____

SOCKS

"Where are my socks?" I asked my mom.

"Have you looked in your drawer?" asked Mom.

I looked in my drawer. The socks were not inside my drawer.

"Have you seen my socks?" I asked my dad.

"Did you look under your bed?" he said.

I searched under my bed. My socks were not under there.

"Have you seen my socks?" I asked my sister.

"Try looking in the bathroom," said my sister.

My socks were not in the bathroom. They were not under the sink. They were not on the floor.

"Do you know where I put my socks?" I asked my brother.

"Look in the car," he said.

I lifted the trunk. I looked under the seats. I looked in the glove box. The socks were not in the car.

"Have you seen my socks?" I asked Grandma. She laughed. "It looks like they are on your back!"

My mom laughed. My dad laughed. My socks were stuck on my shirt.

"Must be the tricky dryer!" said my mother. "Just that tricky dryer!"

We all laughed.

STORY QUESTIONS

1. Who didn't the little girl ask to help her find the socks?
   a. Dad
   b. Grandma
   c. Grandpa
   d. her sister

2. How do you think the little girl felt when she was trying to find her socks?
   a. sad
   b. upset
   c. funny
   d. excited

3. Where were the missing socks?
   a. on the back of her shirt
   b. in the bathroom
   c. on the floor
   d. under the bed

DAILY Warm-Up 8

Name _____ Date _____

SURPRISE!

Curt got up early on Sunday. The sun was out, so he opened his window. It felt nice. The sun was warm on his face. He thought about what he wanted to do today.

"Curt, time for breakfast," called his mom.

He ran down the stairs.

"Yum, bacon and eggs," he said.

"Bacon, eggs, and French toast," said Mom.

"I love French toast," said Curt. "I love bacon and eggs. It is my best breakfast."

"I know you do," said Mom. "Aren't you forgetting something?"

"No, I don't think so," said Curt. The kitchen was very quiet. No one else was around. "What did I forget? Are we going somewhere? Do my clothes look funny? Is my hair a mess?"

"Surprise!" yelled my father after he blew on the birthday horn.

"Surprise!" yelled my sister. She threw colored paper up in the air.

"Surprise!" yelled the baby. She pulled off her party hat.

"Happy Birthday," said my mother. "I made your best breakfast."

"Happy Birthday!" yelled my family.

"What a great surprise," I said.

STORY QUESTIONS

1. How do you think Curt felt when he woke up?
   a. angry   c. happy
   b. sad   d. tired

2. Why do you think Mom made bacon, eggs, and French toast for Curt?
   a. She liked to make them.
   b. He did not like them at all, so she wanted to make them for him.
   c. That was what he liked best.

3. What did Curt forget?
   a. to brush his teeth   c. to do his hair
   b. his birthday   d. to wash his face

DAILY Warm-Up 9   Name _____   Date _____

THE CASE OF THE MISSING KEYS

It was time for school. Mom was in the car. The baby was in the car. I was in the car. Dad was not in the car.

He came out of the house. His face was all red. "Have you seen the car keys?"

I shook my head. Mom shook her head. The baby shook his head.

"Have you seen the car keys?" Dad asked again.

Mom got out of the car. I got out of the car. I took the baby out of his car seat.

"We will help you look for the keys," said Mom. "I am sure one of us will find them in the house."

I looked in the bathroom and under Dad's bed. Mom looked in the pockets of his pants and on his desk.

The baby went right to his bed. He picked up his blanket, and he picked up his pillow. He picked up Dad's keys.

"Dad!" I yelled. "The baby had the keys under his pillow!"

"Thanks, son, for your help! Now, let's race to the car so you are not late for school!"

STORY QUESTIONS

1. Why is the family late?
   a. The keys to the car are missing.
   b. The baby is crying.
   c. Mom is not in the car.
   d. The author was not in the car.

2. Where were the keys to the car?
   a. on Dad's desk
   b. in the car
   c. under the baby's pillow
   d. in Dad's pocket

3. How is this story like most families?
   a. Sometimes they lose the keys to the car.
   b. Sometimes they like to race cars.
   c. Sometimes they eat out at fast food places.

DAILY Name _____ Date _____
Warm-Up 10

THE CAT HAS MY TONGUE!

I woke up this morning. I was not feeling good. My head hurt, and my eyes felt like glue. There was green stuff in my nose. I was sure I was getting sick.

My mom came in to wake me up, "Time to get out of bed, Sweet Pea."

I nodded. I tried to smile, but my mouth was not working. I rolled over and groaned.

"Are you okay?" my mom asked.

I gave her those sad eyes. My mouth opened, but nothing came out.

"Sweet Pea, what is the matter with you. You do not look good. I think something is very wrong."

I shook my head. Grabbing a pencil I wrote her a note. This is what it said.

Mom,

I think I am sick. My eyes hurt and my tongue is broken.

Can you get me a new tongue at the store?

Mom laughed. She sat on my bed. She laughed again.

"What is so funny?" I wrote.

"I guess it is time to go to the doctor. It looks like the cat has your tongue!" she said. We both smiled.

STORY QUESTIONS

1. What is wrong with the little girl in the story?
   a. She is playing sick.
   b. She's not feeling good.
   c. She has a test and wants to stay home from school.
   d. She is mad at her mom.

2. What does the phrase "It looks like the cat has your tongue" mean?
   a. She gave her tongue to the cat for the day.
   b. The cat took her tongue at night.
   c. She doesn't feel good enough to talk.
   d. She wants to get up and dance in circles.

3. What is the name that the mom calls the little girl?
   a. Honey   c. Pumpkin
   b. Sweetheart   d. Sweet Pea

DAILY Name _____ Date _____

Warm-Up 11

THE MISSING DOG

Today is my first day on this job. My name is Booker T. My friends call me Big B for short. I am a detective. Someday I want to be famous. For now, I work for my friends.

This morning I had a knock at my door. I went to see who was there. It was my friend, Karen. She looked sad. She looked like something was wrong.

"Come in," I said. "Are you okay?"

"Of course, I am not okay! That is why I am here to see you," she said. Her face was getting very red.

"Are you hot?" I asked.

"Not hardly," she said. "I just need you to solve a mystery for me."

"I am here to serve," I said with a smile.

She poured out the whole story. It seems someone had stolen her dog. It was a greyhound. His name was Jeb. He was the fastest dog on the block.

I listened to the whole story. "Do you have any leads?" I asked.

"None," she said. "Just these dog biscuits I found in the front yard."

"That will be a good place to start," I said. I grabbed my jacket and hat.

"Do you need anything else?" she asked.

"I will bring my trusty magnifying glass and my notebook," I said. "Let's get on the trail before it gets cold!"

STORY QUESTIONS

1. Who asks Booker T. for his help?
   a. Jeb
   b. a dog
   c. Karen
   d. Big B

2. What do you think will happen next?
   a. Booker T. will find the dog.
   b. Booker T. will eat lunch.
   c. Booker T. will play in the park.
   d. Booker T. will call his dad.

3. What do you think a detective does?
   a. finds paper on the ground
   b. finds clues and answers to why and how things went wrong
   c. looks for missing dogs and cats

BROCCOLI

It was early in the morning. The sun was coming in my window. It was so warm on my face.

"Time to open the shades," I heard myself say out loud.

I pulled back the shades. My eyes just about popped out of my head.

"Is this real?" I asked myself. "Yes, it is real!"

I looked again. I closed my eyes. It was still there. The backyard was full of giant pieces of broccoli. They were as big as my house. They were green with large tops. The tops looked like they needed a lawn mover.

"Mom!" I yelled. "Please come to my room!"

She came up the stairs. Mom went to the window. She looked at the broccoli. "Wow," she said. "Wow! Wow! Wow! Wow!"

"There is broccoli everywhere!" I said.

"I know," she said, "but it is huge. It is scary, and it is growing on top of my garden."

"Whom are you going to call, Mom?"

"I think I will call Broccoli Busters. What do you think?"

"I think that is a good plan. Can I go back to bed?"

"Not today. We are going to have to find some way of getting rid of this broccoli. You know how dad feels about the yard. It will have to go somewhere else!"

STORY QUESTIONS

1. What strange thing was outside the window?
   a. birds
   b. trees
   c. large broccoli
   d. mailbox

2. Whom does Mom plan on calling to help get rid of the broccoli?
   a. Ghost Busters
   b. Apple Busters
   c. Broccoli Busters
   d. Carrot Busters

3. Which **compound word** in the story means "a place in the back of your house that is outside"?
   a. backbone
   b. bedroom
   c. backyard

DAILY Warm-Up 13

Name _____ Date _____

LOOK AT ITS HAIR!

Bonnie came home from work. Her dog did not run out to meet her. It did not lick her face. It did not come to her room. Something was not right.

Her house was very quiet. There was no music. There were no children playing. The TV was not on. Something was very wrong.

She looked in the bedroom. Nothing. She looked outside. No children anywhere. She picked up her cell phone. She called her husband's number. The line went dead.

Bonnie was not feeling very happy. Something had to be wrong. What could it be?

Suddenly, she saw a note on the table. This is what the note said:

> Mom,
>
> We had to take the dog to the groomer. He needed a haircut. He needed a haircut, because someone at our house cut his hair in a new way. We hope the groomer can make the dog look okay. If not, we will call him Patches until it grows out!
>
> Love,
> The Kids and Dad

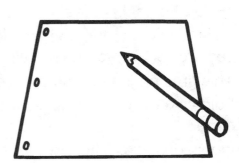

STORY QUESTIONS

1. Why is the house so quiet?
   a. They are hiding.
   b. No one is home.
   c. The family is at the beach.
   d. They are planning a surprise party.

2. What is the new name they are going to give the dog if the groomer cannot fix the hair?
   a. Circles
   b. Squares
   c. Patches
   d. Ovals

3. Who is Bonnie?
   a. the grandpa
   b. the sister
   c. the dad
   d. the mom

DAILY
Warm-Up 14

Name _____ Date _____

GREAT BALLS OF FIRE!

"Great balls of fire!" I heard the old man yell. He was sitting in the park. Next to him was a shopping cart. It was full of junk. His name was Henry. I saw him on my way home from school every day.

"Hi, Henry!" I called.

He waved. "How are you, Hester Sue? Great balls of fire!" he yelled again.

"How was your day, Henry?" I called.

"Same as yesterday," he said. "Great balls of fire!"

"Are you okay?" I asked.

"Sure," he said. "Great balls of fire!"

I walked over to the bench. I looked at his cart. It had the same stuff in it from yesterday. "Do you need help, Henry?" I asked.

This time he jumped up and yelled, "Great balls of fire! Great balls of fire!"

I didn't know what to do, so I just sat down on the bench. He sat down and took off his shoe.

I looked inside. There was a small, <u>sharp</u> rock. It was stuck in his sock. "Let me take that out," I said.

He said, "Sure thing."

I took out the rock. It was sharp. "It would hurt real bad if it was in my shoe," I said.

"Great balls of fire!" I said.

Henry smiled. "Now you see what I was talking about!"

STORY QUESTIONS

1. Why did the man keep saying, "Great balls of fire!"?
    a. He liked the words.   c. He had a rock in his sock.
    b. He wanted to get a sandwich.

2. An **antonym** is a word that means the opposite. *Sharp* is an antonym for . . .
    a. pointed.   c. prickly.
    b. spiky.   d. dull.

3. Why did the author write this story?
    a. to make you laugh   c. to teach you to cook a new dish
    b. to make you cry

DAILY Name _____ Date _____
Warm-Up 1

CANDY PLANET

"We've landed," said John. He hopped out of the spaceship.
"Where are we?" asked Fred. "It looks strange."
"The map says Candy Planet. Let's look around."
The boys shut the door and started walking.
"The sidewalks are chocolate," said John. "Look, the
letters H-E-R-S-H-E-Y are on the path."
"What does H-E-R-S-H-E-Y spell?"
"It spells Hershey. Like Hershey's® chocolate."
"Mmmm. Can we eat the sidewalk?"
"I don't think so," said Fred.
They kept walking. They saw tall buildings. They were made from the biggest candy
bars anybody has ever seen. On some buildings, there were peanuts for windows.
Caramel was painted on some the doors. Gum was used to keep the parts of the
building together.
The city life was filled with candy. Streetlights had red, green, and yellow gumdrops on
them. Cars were all shapes and sizes. Some were made out of chocolate, some were
made out of mint candies, and some were made out of jellybeans. The tires on the
cars were Life Savers®. The people had different kinds of licorice pieces for their hair.
Some people had red licorice, and others had black licorice.
"This is great," said John.
"This makes my teeth hurt," said Fred.
The boys looked up in the sky. There were marshmallows for clouds. All of a sudden,
it started to rain chocolate drops. They ran quickly back to the spaceship.
"Time to go home!"

STORY QUESTIONS

1. Where are the boys?
   a. on a planet made of candy   c. on a planet made of dirt
   b. on a planet made of metal   d. on a planet made of rocks

2. Which one would be a problem on this planet?
   a. cold weather   c. hot weather
   b. bad teeth   d. sticky hands

3. If chocolate drops were falling like rain, you might get . . .
   a. a bad toothache.   b. a headache.   c. a pain in your shoe.

DAILY Name _____ Date _____

Warm-Up 2

WAFFLEHEAD

"Help! I'm being chased by a waffle!" Amber screamed.

"You are being chased by a what?" I asked.

"I am being chased by a big, fat waffle!" yelled Amber.

"Wafflehead! Wafflehead!" screamed the other kids.

I, Ashley, stopped fast. I looked down at my feet. Waffle feet. I looked at my arms. Waffle arms. I looked at my body. It was like a waffle, too.

"Do I still have hair?" I asked Amber.

"Only a little."

"Can you still see my eyes?"

"Only a little, but they are flat and long."

"Is my body flat in the front and flat in the back?"

"Yes," she said, "You look just like a big waffle."

"Help, me, Amber. Take me to the nurse."

"I will," said Amber, "if someone does not eat you first."

We tried to walk to the nurse.

Kids tried to bite me. They tried to pull on my legs. They tried to rip off a part of my waffle. It was not pretty. It did not feel good.

The nurse called 911. She said I looked strange. I had to go home. I had to go to bed. Maybe I will be back to myself in the morning.

STORY QUESTIONS

1. Why were the kids calling Ashley "Wafflehead"?
   a. She was long and flat.
   b. She looked like a waffle.
   c. She had waffle feet.
   d. all of these.

2. What was Ashley hoping she would be in the morning?
   a. someone else   c. a nurse
   b. herself   d. a doctor

3. What did kids try to do to her at school?
   a. They tried to eat her.
   b. They tried to play tetherball with her.
   c. They tried to play soccer with her.

Name _____ Date _____

ARNIE THE ANT

Arnie the ant woke up one rainy day. The water was dripping outside his window. Drip. Drip. Drip.

Today was the big day at the fair. All of his friends were going.

Sammy, Frannie, and Janie would be there. They had planned to eat popcorn. They had planned to eat cotton candy.

Drip. Drip. Drip. He pulled the blanket back over his head.

"That rain had to spoil everything."

Rrrrrring. Rrrrrring. It was the phone. Arnie hopped up to get it. He put on his slippers.

"Hello."

"Hello, Arnie. It's me, Sammy. Did you see the rain?"

"I did, and it makes me mad."

"I have an idea. It is not raining in the desert."

"Okay."

"So, let's pack a lunch and go to the desert. We can climb on the hills. Frannie and Janie could bring their bikes. We could eat chicken. It would be warm."

"What a great idea. Can you call the others?"

"I will. We will pick you up in an hour," said Sammy.

"Okay," said Arnie, "but if it stops raining, let's go to the fair tomorrow."

STORY QUESTIONS

1. What made the ants change their plans for the day?

    a. snow   c. sunshine

    b. rain   d. clouds

2. How are the animals like most people when the weather changed their plans?

    a. They were too sad to do anything at all.

    b. They sat down and cried.

    c. They made a new plan.

3. What was the new plan?

    a. go to the desert and eat lunch   c. play in the rain

    b. stay home and rent a movie   d. eat cotton candy

DAILY Warm-Up 4

Name _____ Date _____

TALKING SHAMPOO BOTTLE

Let's get this straight. I am a bottle of shampoo. My name is Andria. It is my job to make a mess in the bathroom.

Everyday I have the same old job. Wash the hair. Wash the hair. Wash the hair.

Sometimes Jen is late, but she always washes her hair. She likes to have it clean and shiny, but she does not care about me.

I will show her who is boss! Tonight she came to wash her hair. She got a big surprise. I started talking to her. The story went like this.

"Hey, what are you doing?"

Jen looked around the bathroom. "Who is talking to me?"

"It's me, the shampoo bottle. My name is Andria."

"Wait. Are you telling me a shampoo bottle talks? No way. I don't believe it!"

"It's true. I am talking to you."

Jen looked in the cupboards. She opened the doors under the sink. "Shampoo bottles don't talk."

"Well, I do. I just have five words for you!"

"Well, if you are talking, what are the five words?"

"Stop squeezing me so hard!"

STORY QUESTIONS

1. Who is telling this story?
- a. Jen
- b. a bar of soap
- c. a bottle of shampoo
- d. a hair dryer

2. How do you think Jen felt when she heard Andria talking?
- a. mad
- b. surprised
- c. sad
- d. excited

3. What did Andria tell Jen?
- a. "Stop using so much shampoo!"
- b. "Stop making so many bubbles!"
- c. "Stop squeezing me so hard!"
- d. "Leave me under the sink!"

DAILY Warm-Up 5

Name _____ Date _____

WISHES

Have you ever wanted to have someone else's feet? I have. My sister has tiny feet. Mine are big. Very big! She has size 2, and I have size 6. I always have wanted my sister's feet.

Today when I went to put on my shoes, they did not fit. My feet slipped right in and right back out. What was wrong with me?

I looked at the shoes. They were mine. I tried again. Too big. In fact, they looked like clown shoes. Maybe it was the laces. I tied the laces tighter. No use. The shoes were still too big.

I heard a scream from my sister's room. Mom and I both ran to her room. She was crying on the floor. Jessica was holding her feet. They were huge. She was looking at her shoes.

"Mom," she said, "I got <u>monster</u> feet last night! My shoes don't fit. What am I going to do?"

Mom said, "I don't know. Do your feet hurt?"

I looked at my feet. I looked at Jessie's feet. An idea came to me. I ran to my bedroom and got my shoes. She gave me her shoes. We put them on. We both looked funny.

I didn't want to tell her what had happened. All I can say is I hope all my other wishes do not come true!

STORY QUESTIONS

1. Why did the author want her sister's feet?
   a. They were big.   c. They were small.
   b. They were long.   d. They were ugly.

2. Synonyms are words that mean the same thing. *Monster* is a synonym for . . .
   a. little.   c. small.
   b. tiny.   d. huge.

3. What did the author learn?
   a. She still wanted all the things she wanted.
   b. She hoped all of her wishes would not come true after all.
   c. She hoped three of her wishes would come true.

Name _____   Date _____

MR. CAT

Mr. Cat had a store. He sold candy and ice cream. The store had paper and cans. It had chicken and ham. It had everything you needed.

All the children in the neighborhood came to buy things from him. They came to see Mr. Cat. All of the children loved him. He would smile and say nice things.

He always wore a tall hat. The hat was green. It had a black ribbon on top. It had seven blue buttons on the side. They were put on with glue.

Every day children would bring him new things for his hat. He had a feather from Mattie and a stone from Jenny. Emily gave him a pencil, and Stuart gave him a piece of gum. He glued everything on his hat.

One night his hat fell off his head. It fell on the floor. It was too heavy. It had too many things. Mr. Cat sat and cried.

"What will I do?" he asked the children.

"I have an idea," said Kacey. "I think you should put the hat on the wall. Buy a new hat and glue on more things. You could have many hats. You could keep them on the wall for everyone to see."

"What a great idea," said Mr. Cat. "That is just what I will do."

STORY QUESTIONS

1. What words can we use to talk about Mr. Cat?
   a. kind, caring, nice to everyone   c. wicked and tall
   b. mean and nasty   d. short and mean

2. The children always gave Mr. Cat . . .
   a. sodas.   c. big gifts.
   b candy.   d. small gifts.

3. How did Kacey help Mr. Cat?
   a. She helped him sell candy and ice cream.
   b. She brought more friends to his store.
   c. She told him to put his heavy hat on the wall.

DAILY Warm-Up 7 Name _____ Date _____

WATERPARK

"Hey, look at me!" yelled Roxie, the big red dog. She was going down the slide at the waterpark.

"Wait for me!" yelled her sister, Colleen.

"I'm on my way!" screamed Gary. He was a small, brown dog.

The three dogs laughed and slid down the huge water slide.

Two times. Three times. Four times.

"Time for lunch!" yelled Roxie's mother. "Come and eat!"

Roxie, Colleen, and Gary got off the slide. They took their towels. They picked up their glasses. They put on their flip-flops.

"Lunch. Oh boy! Am I hungry!" said Roxie.

"Me, too," said Gary. "What did your mom bring to eat?"

"She has pizza and soda," said Colleen.

"I love pizza," said Gary. "Is it cheese?"

"I think it is pepperoni," she said.

"Pepperoni is good, but cheese is better," said Gary.

The three dogs saw their mother. She was waving at them. She had three plates.

"What kind of pizza would you like?" she asked. "I have pepperoni and cheese."

"I'll have pepperoni," said Colleen.

"We'll both have cheese," said Gary and Roxie at the same time.

STORY QUESTIONS

1. Where are the children for the day?
   a. basketball courts
   b. waterpark
   c. baseball park
   d. soccer field

2. How do you think the dogs felt going down the slide?
   a. scared
   b. surprised
   c. mad
   d. excited

3. What kind of pizza do Gary and Roxie like best?
   a. pepperoni
   b. sausage
   c. pepperoni and cheese
   d. cheese

THE MOON

Our class wanted to go on a field trip. Our teacher, Mr. F, said our class could go.

"Where do you want to go?" he asked.

"I want to go to the zoo," said John.

"I want to go to the park," said Lisa.

We all wanted to go many places. He wrote the list on the board—zoo, park, and beach.

Jenna raised her hand, "I want to go to the moon."

We all laughed. Only astronauts go to the moon.

"We will keep it a secret," said Mr. F. "If we are to go on this trip, we all have to work hard. We all have to do chores. We all have to bring money."

"Okay," we said.

Tommy cleaned the yard. Sally swept the floor. Lisa scrubbed the bathroom. John cleaned the doors. We all brought our money to Mr. F.

The day before the field trip, he told us to pack a bag. "Bring a toothbrush, toothpaste, and two pairs of pants. You will need a jacket and two shirts. Be ready by 7 A.M. Meet me at the school."

We were all at school early with our bags. Mr. F. was there, too.

"Where are we going?" I asked.

He smiled, "We're going on a field trip to the moon!"

STORY QUESTIONS

1. Where is Mr. F's class going?
   a. on a day trip to the museum
   b. on a trip to the grocery store
   c. on a field trip to the moon
   d. on a picnic to the park

2. What do astronauts do?
   a. walk in space
   b. ride in spaceships
   c. wear helmets
   d. all of these

3. How did they make money to go on the trip?
   a. The asked their parents to give money.
   b. They did chores.
   c. They ran around the school.

DAILY Warm-Up 9

Name _____ Date _____

MORE CHILI AND CHEESE, PLEASE!

Brooke was a little girl. She lived with her mom. They had a one-story house. Brooke liked school. She did not love homework.

Everyday she ate chili and cheese. Everything had to have chili and cheese.

She ate potatoes. She wanted chili and cheese.

Brooke had a burger. She wanted to add chili and cheese.

Brooke ate chili and cheese on toast. She ate chili and cheese in soup.

Brooke ate chili and cheese on spaghetti. She ate chili and cheese on her ice cream.

She just loved chili and cheese.

One day Mom and Brooke went out to eat.

Brooke always asked, "May I have chili and cheese?" Then she said, "Mom, please try one bite of chili and cheese."

No one wanted to try it. No one wanted to eat chili and cheese.

Her mom said, "No way!" But, she took a bite anyway.

Mom yelled, "I want more chili and cheese!"

STORY QUESTIONS

1. What did Brooke want to eat on everything?
   a. chili and cheese   c. spaghetti
   b. fries   d. toast

2. What happened when Mom tried chili and cheese?
   a. She hated it.
   b. She liked it.
   c. She said it was okay.
   d. She gave the chili and cheese to Brooke.

3. This story is told in . . .
   a. third person
   b. first person
   c. fifth person

DAILY Warm-Up 10

Name _____ Date _____

STAR GAZING

"I want to go to the circus on Saturday," said Molly. "Mom, will you take me?"

"I don't know if we can go. I have to go to work," she said.

"I was thinking that it would be fun to see the clowns," said Molly.

"I might have to work," said Mom.

"The animals will be loud," said Molly.

"I think I have to go to work," said Mom.

"The popcorn will taste like butter," said Molly.

"Molly, look at me. I HAVE TO WORK!"

"Cotton candy will be pink and fluffy," said Molly.

Mom stopped. She looked at Molly. "Oh, no," she said.

"What is wrong?" asked Molly.

"You have stars in your eyes," said Mom.

"Huh?" said Molly.

"You did not hear me. You have stars in your eyes. I see a circus. I see animals. There are yellow balls in your eyes! I cannot go to work. We will go to the circus!"

STORY QUESTIONS

1. Which of these will not be at the circus that Molly wants to go to?

    a. homework   c. clowns

    b. cotton candy   d. animals

2. Why didn't Molly's mother think she could go with her?

    a. She didn't want to.

    b. She had to work.

    c. She was hungry.

    d. She said it cost too much money.

3. Molly's mother said, "You have stars in your eyes." What did she mean by this?

    a. Molly had real stars in her eyes.

    b. Molly had dust in her eyes.

    c. Molly really wanted to see stars.

    d. Molly really wanted to go the circus.

Name _____   Date _____

CANDICE

My name is Candice, and I am a toaster. My home is in the kitchen, but not for very long.

I found out some very exciting news about me. Suzi is going to college, and she is taking me with her. I have always wanted to go to college. I have always wanted to travel.

I found out all about it last night. Suzi and her mom came to the kitchen, and they had a talk.

"Hey, Suzi, what do you think about traveling? Do you want to see the world? Do you want to go to college?"

Suzi nodded her head. "Yes, I want to go! When do I leave? What will I do? What things will I see?"

"I don't know what you will see," said her mother. "I do know some things. You will need to take some things with you. You can take my toaster to cook waffles and toast. If you want English muffins, you can cook them in the toaster, too."

"What else do I need? Will you leave me alone? Will the city be big?"

"You will stay in a small room with another girl. I will stay with you for awhile, but then you will be on your own."

Suzi then became sad thinking about not seeing her mom. Little does she know that I will talk to her and keep her company while I cook her waffles and toast!

STORY QUESTIONS

1. Candice is a . . .
   a. toaster.
   b. oven.
   c. pan.
   d. glass.

2. Where is Candice going?
   a. to the dance studio.
   b. to get a tattoo.
   c. to the nail shop.
   d. to college.

3. Why did the author write this?
   a. to tell you a silly story that cannot be true
   b. to tell you facts about toasters
   c to make you want to buy a toaster

DAILY Name _____ Date _____
Warm-Up 12

A LOLLIPOP?

Last Tuesday I woke up late. My clock did not work, and Mom did not wake me up. It was a strange day.

When I got out of bed, I went plop, right in the middle of the floor. I got up. Plop! I fell again. I looked down. My feet had turned into a stick. My feet were one, long white, cardboard stick.

I bounced to the mirror. My head was a lollipop. It was a big, round, cherry lollipop. I was a sucker!

"Help! Mom! Help!"

Mom came running to my room. She sat on my bed. Mom laughed and laughed. She could not stop laughing. Mom laughed until she cried.

"Where is my Candice and what have you done with her?" she asked.

"I am Candice," I said.

"You sound like Candice," said Mom.

"I am Candice," I said.

"You smell like Candice," said Mom. "Okay, Candice, change back to the little girl I once knew."

Poof! In a flash I was back to normal. Thank goodness for moms!

STORY QUESTIONS

1. Who is telling this story?
   a. Candice   c. her dad
   b. Mom   d. Candice's brother

2. Why was Candice so upset?
   a. She thought she became a tree.   c. She thought she was sick.
   b. She thought she broke her leg.   d. She became a lollipop.

3. Who saved Candice?
   a. Candice's brother   c. No one
   b. Mom

MARTIANS

A loud noise hit the roof. Sandy jumped out of bed. Her head hit the top of the bed. She got a big bump. Her slippers were missing.

"Ouch! What was that noise?" she asked.

Bump. Bump. Thud. The noise came again. Sandy went to the window. She tried to open it. She pushed and pushed. It would not open.

Sandy went to the door of her house. She tried to open it. She pushed and pushed. It would not open.

"Whatever is the matter?" She went to the phone. She called her mother.

Her mother was sleeping. She woke up when the phone rang.

"Hello."

"Mother, something is <u>outside</u> the house. I cannot open the windows or doors."

"Look through the glass. I think there are huge Martians with wings on their backs outside," said Mother. "Show them a big smile and see if they are friendly."

Sandy went to the window and saw one of the Martians. She smiled really big and watched to see what they would do.

One Martian flew to the window and opened it for Sandy. Then he flew to the door and opened it. He shook her hand and then flew back to the top of the roof where his spaceship was parked.

"Wow! Martians can be friendly and helpful!" Sandy said to herself.

STORY QUESTIONS

1. This is a made up story about giant . . .

    a. monsters.   c. ghosts.

    b. dinosaurs.   d. Martians.

2. Antonyms are words that mean the opposite. The antonym for *outside* is . . .

    a. house.   c. scissors.

    b. inside.   d. windows.

3. How did Sandy get out of the house?

    a. A Martian helped her.

    b. Her mother helped her.

    c. Sandy opened the doors and windows herself.

Name _____ Date _____

JELLYBEANS AND ME

"Hey, Buster, come look out the window," said my brother.

"Why?" I asked. My new book was too good. It was called *Jellybeans and Me.*

"Come here now!" he yelled. "You have to see this."

I put my book down on the couch. I walked to the window to look outside.

"What is it?" I asked.

"Look outside. Look next door."

"Holy Cow! Mom, come and look outside!" I yelled.

"Oh, my," said Mom. "We should call the police right away." She went to the phone to dial 911.

"Hello," said the voice.

"Hello," said my mother. "I think you had better come to our house right away."

"What is wrong?" asked the voice. "How can I help?"

"There are jellybeans next door. They are blue, green, and yellow. They have legs, arms, and heads. These jellybeans have eyes and hats. I can see a big moving van. It looks like they are moving into the house next door. They have many boxes and bags."

"Do they look dangerous?"

"I don't know. They are just jellybeans."

"Lady, are you okay? Do you have a fever? Do you need a doctor?" the voice asked.

"Yes, I think I am okay. Please come now! I don't want neighbors that are jellybeans," said mother.

I smiled.

STORY QUESTIONS

1. Why did the police think the call was not real?
   a. Jellybeans are everywhere.
   b. Jellybeans do not move into houses.
   c. Jellybeans are our friends.
   d. Jellybeans are always moving.

2. What book is the author reading?
   a. *Jellybeans and Me*
   b. *Jellybeans and You*
   c. *Jellybeans and Us*
   d. *Jellybeans and We*

3. How do you think the book will help the family?
   a. It won't.
   b. It will help them know how to shop for jellybeans.
   c. It will tell them how to cook jellybeans.
   d. It will help them to know how jellybean people act.

DAILY Name _____ Date _____
Warm-Up 15

VANISHING VEGGIES

Tuesdays are strange at my house. My mom doesn't think so, but I know that it is true.

Every day my mom always fixes dinner. She always fixes me veggies. She always makes me eat beans. She makes me eat corn. She makes me eat carrots. They are veggies, and I hate veggies.

Every night she puts the veggies on my plate. But for some strange reason, on Tuesdays they just disappear. They just go away a little at a time. I do not know where they go, but they go. I wiggle my nose. Some veggies go away. I clap my hands. A few more veggies go away. I smile at my mom, and even more veggies go away.

My mom gets mad. She says, "Sarah, where are your veggies?"

I smile, "They are gone, Mom. They have disappeared."

"Where did they go?"

"I do not know where they went. They just went away."

She says, "Well then, I will have to give you some more."

I say, "That is okay. Today is Tuesday, and they will just go away. Give me more, Mom!"

Mom gives me more, and they start to go away. My mother does not see them disappear. I cannot see where they go.

She says, "Tuesdays are so strange. I think we will eat fruit on Tuesdays."

"I love fruit," I said. "Tuesdays will be the best days of all!"

STORY QUESTIONS

1. Why happens to Sarah's veggies on Tuesdays?
   a. They dance on her plate.   c. They swim over her plate.
   b. They hide under her plate.   d. They disappear off her plate.

2. What does Mom decide to do?
   a. stare at her veggies   c. buy veggies off the truck
   b. give her less veggies   d. give her fruit on Tuesdays

3. Which one is **NOT** a fact that happens in the story on Tuesdays?
   a. She claps her hands. The veggies go away.
   b. She wiggles her nose. The veggies go away.
   c. She eats the veggies that are on her plate.
   d. Mom says, "Sarah, where are your veggies?"

DAILY Name _____ Date _____
Warm-Up 16

SOLDIERS UNDER MY BED

Bang! Bang! Bang!

I woke up with a start. What was that noise? I lay very still. My ears were open wide.

Bang! Bang! Bang!

"What is that noise?" I asked myself.

"It is the soldiers under your bed. They play war at night," said my teddy bear.

I sat up in bed. "Are you talking to me, Mr. Teddy Bear?"

"I am. Look under your bed. The soldiers fight at night. Didn't you hear them before?"

"No. I was sleeping at night."

"Look and see," said Mr. Teddy Bear. "But do not let them see you!"

I put my head over the bed. The soldiers were lying on the floor. They had their guns in their hands. They were fighting and rolling. It was amazing. Their voices sounded tiny. They were shouting and yelling.

I sat up. "Mr. Teddy Bear, do they always fight at night?" I asked.

"Most of the time. They want the toy box. The team that wins gets to sleep under there."

"Wow," I said. "Soldiers fighting over a toy box. Who would have guessed?"

STORY QUESTIONS

1. How do you think the child felt when he heard the noise?
a. brave
b. scared
c. mad
d. sad

2. What made the noise?
a. a ball bouncing
b. tiny soldiers fighting
c. mother knocking on the door
d. tree branches blowing against the window

3. What were they fighting about?
a. who gets to play with Mr. Teddy Bear
b. who gets to jump on the toy box
c. who would sleep under the toy box
d. who would get to play outside

ANSWER KEY

Answer Key

Nonfiction

Animals

Page 9 The Giraffe
1. b
2. c
3. b

Page 10 Cats
1. c
2. d
3. a

Page 11 Squid
1. c
2. d
3. a

Page 12 Puffins
1. b
2. c
3. a

Page 13 Saola
1. a
2. d
3. c

Page 14 Mole Rat
1. a
2. d
3. b

Page 15 Tiger
1. c
2. c
3. a

Page 16 Lions
1. c
2. a
3. b

Page 17 Red Squirrel
1. a
2. d
3. b

Page 18 Night Animals
1. a
2. b
3. d

Page 19 Chipmunk
1. d
2. c
3. a

Page 20 Sharks
1. a
2. d
3. c

Page 21 Hermit Crab
1. c
2. a
3. b

Page 22 Tongues
1. b
2. c
3. c

Page 23 Groundhogs
1. c
2. a
3. b

Page 24 Seahorses
1. d
2. a
3. d

Page 25 Ostrich
1. a
2. c
3. b

Page 26 Hummingbirds
1. c
2. a
3. b

Biography

Page 27 George Washington
1. a
2. c
3. b

Page 28 Betsy Ross
1. b
2. d
3. c

Page 29 Thomas Jefferson
1. b
2. a
3. c

Page 30 Dolley Madison
1. d
2. b
3. a

Page 31 Albert Einstein
1. c
2. b
3. d

Page 32 George W. Bush
1. d
2. c
3. b

Page 33 Michelle Kwan
1. b
2. c
3. a

Page 34 Tiger Woods
1. b
2. a
3. d

Page 35 Condoleeza Rice
1. c
2. a
3. c

Answer Key

Page 36 Walt Disney
1. b
2. c
3. d

Page 37 Denzel Washington
1. a
2. b
3. d

Page 38 Sandra Bullock
1. a
2. b
3. d

Page 39 Bruce Willis
1. c
2. a
3. b

Page 40 Laura Bush
1. b
2. c
3. a

Page 41 Babe Ruth
1. c
2. b
3. b

Page 42 Hank Aaron
1. a
2. b
3. b

Page 43 Christopher Columbus
1. c
2. d
3. c

Page 44 Harriet Tubman
1. c
2. d
3. b

American History

Page 45 Airplane
1. c
2. d
3. a

Page 46 Cell Phones
1. b
2. c
3. a

Page 47 Coke
1. d
2. a
3. c

Page 48 The Iron
1. c
2. a
3. d

Page 49 The Popsicle
1. c
2. a
3. b

Page 50 Light Bulbs
1. c
2. a
3. b

Page 51 Kool-Aid
1. d
2. a
3. b

Page 52 Marshmallows
1. d
2. a
3. a

Page 53 Microwave Oven
1. c
2. a
3. b

Page 54 Q-tips
1. b
2. c
3. a

Page 55 Sewing Machine
1. b
2. a
3. d

Page 56 Umbrellas
1. a
2. c
3. d

Page 57 Wipers
1. d
2. a
3. a

Page 58 Band-Aids
1. c
2. a
3. b

Page 59 Basketball
1. b
2. c
3. a

Page 60 The Telephone
1. c
2. a
3. a

Page 61 Braille
1. a
2. c
3. d

Page 62 Diapers
1. c
2. c
3. b

Answer Key

Science

Page 63 Mammals
1. c
2. c
3. b

Page 64 Birds
1. a
2. b
3. b

Page 65 Fish
1. d
2. a
3. b

Page 66 Reptiles
1. b
2. d
3. b

Page 67 Amphibians
1. c
2. c
3. d

Page 68 Insects
1. c
2. c
3. b

Page 69 Seeds
1. d
2. b
3. b

Page 70 Habitats
1. b
2. a
3. c

Page 71 Seasons
1. a
2. c
3. c

Page 72 Earth's Resources
1. c
2. c
3. a

Current Events

Page 73 Winter Olympics
1. b
2. c
3. a

Page 74 iPod
1. c
2. d
3. a

Page 75 Hurricane Katrina
1. a
2. c
3. a

Page 76 Tsunami
1. c
2. d
3. c

Page 77 Tour de France
1. d
2. c
3. b

Page 78 September 11th
1. d
2. b
3. c

Page 79 John Paul II Dies
1. c
2. a
3. d

Page 80 Ben
1. a
2. d
3. a

Page 81 Air Force One
1. d
2. b
3. c

Page 82 Lion King Tryouts
1. c
2. d
3. a

Page 83 Five Mummies
1. d
2. b
3. d

Page 84 Working in the Mines
1. d
2. c
3. d

Page 85 Moms and Dads Want Kids to Eat Veggies
1. c
2. c
3. b

Page 86 Space Shuttle Comes Home
1. a
2. a
3. b

Fiction

Fairy Tales and Folklore

Page 89 Barnella
1. b
2. a
3. b

Page 90 Three Little Bugs
1. d
2. a
3. b

Answer Key

Page 91 Savannah and the Giant Sunflower
1. b
2. a
3. b

Page 92 Tiny, Black Cow
1. d
2. a
3. b

Page 93 The Horses and the Troll
1. a
2. c
3. b

Page 94 Essie and the Parrots
1. d
2. a
3. b

Page 95 Lars and Nina
1. a
2. d
3. b

Page 96 Rain Blue
1. d
2. a
3. c

Page 97 The Rat and the Princess
1. c
2. a
3. d

Page 98 Slow Worm and the Quail
1. b
2. a
3. a

Page 99 Ugly Monkey
1. d
2. d
3. a

Page 100 The Apple Girl
1. b
2. c
3. a

Page 101 Why Bees Buzz
1. d
2. c
3. d

Page 102 Karl and the Talking Kiwi
1. b
2. a
3. b

Page 103 Jumping Jellyfish
1. a
2. c
3. b

Page 104 Little Blue Bonnet
1. b
2. d
3. a

Historical Fiction

Page 105 Sam Walks on the Moon
1. a
2. d
3. b

Page 106 "I Have a Dream"
1. b
2. a
3. a

Page 107 A Pilgrim Day
1. d
2. a
3. b

Page 108 One-Room Schoolhouse
1. a
2. c
3. a

Page 109 Stars in Her Eyes
1. a
2. c
3. c

Page 110 Henry Learns to Fly
1. d
2. d
3. a

Page 111 Grandpa and the Five and Dime
1. b
2. c
3. c

Page 112 Crayons
1. b
2. c
3. a

Page 113 Band-Aids
1. c
2. b
3. b

Page 114 Toll House Cookies
1. b
2. a
3. d

Page 115 The Horseless Carriage
1. c
2. d
3. a

Page 116 Life Savers
1. b
2. a
3. c

Page 117 A Model House
1. c
2. d
3. b

Answer Key

Page 118 The Meat Plant
1. d
2. c
3. a

Page 119 In the Mine
1. c
2. b
3. a

Page 120 Ore Boat on the Great Lakes
1. d
2. c
3. a

Contemporary Realistic Fiction

Page 121 Frank
1. a
2. c
3. b

Page 122 Yucky
1. c
2. a
3. d

Page 123 Hoops
1. b
2. c
3. a

Page 124 The Big Game
1. c
2. a
3. c

Page 125 Missing Money
1. a
2. c
3. b

Page 126 Party
1. c
2. d
3. a

Page 127 Skiing
1. c
2. d
3. a

Page 128 After School
1. b
2. c
3. a

Page 129 Fight
1. d
2. a
3. c

Page 130 My Hair
1. b
2. b
3. d

Page 131 No Homework
1. a
2. c
3. b

Page 132 Best Friends
1. a
2. d
3. c

Page 133 The Big "D"
1. d
2. c
3. d

Page 134 Moving Day
1. b
2. a
3. c

Page 135 Stuck in the Snow Fort
1. a
2. d
3. b

Page 136 The Tent
1. b
2. c
3. b

Mystery/Suspense/ Adventure

Page 137 Lights in the Shed
1. c
2. d
3. a

Page 138 The Bus
1. b
2. c
3. b

Page 139 Snapshot
1. c
2. a
3. c

Page 140 That's My Dog!
1. a
2. c
3. b

Page 141 Who's At My House?
1. c
2. a
3. d

Page 142 Codes
1. a
2. c
3. c

Page 143 Socks
1. c
2. b
3. a

Page 144 Surprise!
1. c
2. c
3. b

Page 145 The Case of the Missing Keys

1. a
2. c
3. a

Page 146 The Cat Has My Tongue!

1. b
2. c
3. d

Page 147 The Missing Dog

1. c
2. a
3. b

Page 148 Broccoli

1. c
2. c
3. c

Page 149 Look at Its Hair!

1. b
2. c
3. d

Page 150 Great Balls of Fire!

1. c
2. d
3. a

Fantasy

Page 151 Candy Planet

1. a
2. c
3. b

Page 152 Wafflehead

1. d
2. b
3. a

Page 153 Arnie the Ant

1. b
2. c
3. a

Page 154 Talking Shampoo Bottle

1. c
2. b
3. c

Page 155 Wishes

1. c
2. d
3. b

Page 156 Mr. Cat

1. a
2. d
3. c

Page 157 Waterpark

1. b
2. d
3. d

Page 158 The Moon

1. c
2. d
3. b

Page 159 More Chili and Cheese, Please!

1. a
2. b
3. a

Page 160 Star Gazing

1. a
2. b
3. d

Page 161 Candice

1. a
2. d
3. a

Page 162 A Lollipop?

1. a
2. d
3. b

Page 163 Martians

1. d
2. b
3. a

Page 164 Jellybeans and Me

1. b
2. a
3. d

Page 165 Vanishing Veggies

1. d
2. d
3. c

Page 166 Soldiers Under My Bed

1. b
2. b
3. c

Leveling Chart

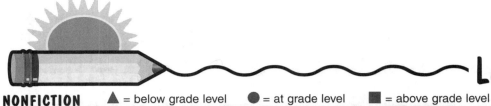

NONFICTION   ▲ = below grade level   ● = at grade level   ■ = above grade level

Animals		Biography		American History		Science		Current Events	
Page 9	●	Page 27	■	Page 45	●	Page 63	●	Page 73	●
Page 10	●	Page 28	●	Page 46	●	Page 64	●	Page 74	●
Page 11	●	Page 29	■	Page 47	●	Page 65	▲	Page 75	●
Page 12	■	Page 30	■	Page 48	●	Page 66	●	Page 76	■
Page 13	●	Page 31	●	Page 49	▲	Page 67	●	Page 77	●
Page 14	●	Page 32	●	Page 50	●	Page 68	●	Page 78	■
Page 15	■	Page 33	●	Page 51	●	Page 69	●	Page 79	●
Page 16	●	Page 34	●	Page 52	■	Page 70	●	Page 80	●
Page 17	●	Page 35	■	Page 53	■	Page 71	●	Page 81	●
Page 18	●	Page 36	●	Page 54	●	Page 72	▲	Page 82	●
Page 19	●	Page 37	●	Page 55	■			Page 83	■
Page 20	●	Page 38	●	Page 56	●			Page 84	●
Page 21	●	Page 39	■	Page 57	●			Page 85	●
Page 22	●	Page 40	●	Page 58	▲			Page 86	■
Page 23	●	Page 41	●	Page 59	■				
Page 24	●	Page 42	■	Page 60	●				
Page 25	●	Page 43	●	Page 61	●				
Page 26	■	Page 44	●	Page 62	■				

FICTION   ▲ = below grade level   ● = at grade level   ■ = above grade level

Fairy Tales and Folklore		Historical Fiction		Contemporary Realistic Fiction		Mystery/Suspense/Adventure		Fantasy	
Page 89	●	Page 105	▲	Page 121	▲	Page 137	▲	Page 151	●
Page 90	▲	Page 106	●	Page 122	▲	Page 138	▲	Page 152	●
Page 91	●	Page 107	●	Page 123	●	Page 139	●	Page 153	●
Page 92	▲	Page 108	●	Page 124	●	Page 140	●	Page 154	●
Page 93	●	Page 109	●	Page 125	●	Page 141	▲	Page 155	▲
Page 94	●	Page 110	●	Page 126	●	Page 142	●	Page 156	●
Page 95	●	Page 111	▲	Page 127	●	Page 143	▲	Page 157	●
Page 96	●	Page 112	●	Page 128	▲	Page 144	■	Page 158	▲
Page 97	●	Page 113	●	Page 129	●	Page 145	▲	Page 159	●
Page 98	●	Page 114	▲	Page 130	▲	Page 146	●	Page 160	●
Page 99	●	Page 115	●	Page 131	●	Page 147	●	Page 161	●
Page 100	■	Page 116	▲	Page 132	▲	Page 148	●	Page 162	●
Page 101	▲	Page 117	●	Page 133	●	Page 149	■	Page 163	■
Page 102	●	Page 118	●	Page 134	▲	Page 150	●	Page 164	●
Page 103	●	Page 119	●	Page 135	●			Page 165	■
Page 104	●	Page 120	●	Page 136	●			Page 166	●

Congratulations
to

_____

for completing

_____

_____

_____
Signature

_____
Date